You Can't SCARE Me...
I Have a
TEENAGER!

A PARENT'S
BASIC SURVIVAL
GUIDE

By DAVID GOLD, PhD, and THOMAS STACY, PhD

Child & Family Press • Washington, DC

Child & Family Press is an imprint of the Child Welfare League of America, Inc. The Child Welfare League of America is the nation's oldest and largest membership-based child welfare organization. We are committed to engaging people everywhere in promoting the well-being of children, youth, and their families, and protecting every child from harm. All proceeds from the sale of this book support CWLA's programs in behalf of children and families.

CHILD WELFARE LEAGUE OF AMERICA, INC.
HEADQUARTERS
440 First Street, NW, Third Floor, Washington, DC 20001-2085
E-mail: books@cwla.org

CURRENT PRINTING (last digit)
10 9 8 7 6 5 4 3 2 1

Cover and text design by Jennifer R. Geanakos
Edited by Tegan A. Culler
Printed in the United States of America
ISBN-13: 978-1-58760-039-5
ISBN-10: 1-58760-039-0

Library of Congress Cataloging-in-Publication Data
Stacy, Thomas W.
    You can't scare me—I have a teenager : a parent's basic survival guide /
    by Thomas W. Stacy and David A. Gold.
        p. cm.
    Summary: "This handbook of techniques for effectively parenting teenagers
    offers parents information on basic adolescent development, communication,
    and discipline. It also includes special chapters on substance abuse, eating
    disorders, sexuality, and depression"—Provided by publisher.
        Includes bibliographical references.
        ISBN-13: 978-1-58760-039-5 (pbk. : alk. paper)
        ISBN-10: 1-58760-039-0 (pbk. : alk. paper)
        1. Parent and teenager. 2. Adolescent psychology.
        3. Adolescence. I. Gold, David A. II. Title.
        HQ799.15.S72 2005
        649'.125--dc22   2005009463

We would like to dedicate this book to our patients and their families, who have taught us as much about parenting as we have taught them. It has been a privilege and a pleasure to work with so many committed and caring parents and adolescents who have come into our offices in pain, anger, and fear and trusted us to help shepherd them through their struggles, crises, and conflicts.

We would also like to dedicate this book to our colleagues who have mentored and collaborated with us throughout our careers.

And finally, we would like to make a special dedication to our own parents, who started the teaching, and to our children, who continue to provide us with an education.

CONTENTS

SECTION THREE
Some Common Hazards You May Encounter

SECTION FOUR
Extreme Environments

SECTION FIVE
Sustaining Survival for the Long Term

We would like to thank our wives, Susan and Jessica, for their support, encouragement, and editing, and for their willingness to take care of anything and everything else while we worked on this project.

We would also like to thank Catherine, Rachel, Joanne, Fred, Cathy, Jean, Paul, Betsy, Andy, and Maxine for their help and input.

And finally, a special thanks to Fatimah for her editing, typing, and running commentary.

Navigation and Finding Your Coordinates

CHAPTER 1

THE MYTHICAL INSTRUCTION MANUAL

Introduction

For a long time, the parents we met through our practice and in our workshops asked us to write a book on parenting teenagers, and for a long time, we resisted. The primary reason for this was that we are psychologists, and as everyone knows, shrinks never give straight answers. This is not because we are a sadistic bunch, but because sometimes there *are* no straight answers. Particularly when it comes to parenting teens, the truth is that it depends: it depends on all the individuals involved, what you have tried that has worked, and what you've tried that hasn't. We never felt entirely comfortable with the idea of describing the causes and solutions for the issues that teens and their parents experience as though there was only one right answer that applied to everyone.

Most parents agree that adolescence is, by far, the most difficult developmental stage to parent. In a perfect world, just as your child began to show the unmistakable signs of puberty, someone would have handed you a detailed instruction manual covering the ideal response for every event and contingency to occur in your family's life during the better part of the decade to come. (And, in a truly perfect world, your brand-new teenager would have come with 24-hour tech support.) Unfortunately, this is not the world we live in.

When we finally decided to take on this project, therefore, we did so with the idea that rather than giving parents the answers (and pretending that those answers would be universal), we would try to give parents a basic survival guide. In this book, we provide general information, strategies, and goals that will allow you to figure out your own answers, address your families' specific issues and needs, and adjust your approach as your family changes. Of course, all adolescents are different and present different challenges. We attempt to speak to some of these differences, equip parents to respond to them effectively, and offer them options for additional support when things seem overwhelming.

Balance

As parents, we are always looking for the right balance. As you will see, balance is one of the ongoing threads that appears throughout this book. It's a central concept to the way in which we view parenting in general and parenting teenagers specifically. You may often find yourself needing to juggle various parenting or communication styles, such as trying to figure out how to find the balance between protecting your teen and allowing them to make their own mistakes and get burned so they learn about consequences themselves. The frustrating part is that the "correct" balance is always changing because teens are always changing. No matter what, however, don't forget that all teens need security and structure, emotional connection, and attachment. If you start from there, you'll find that the balancing act becomes a little easier.

Mistakes

Parents of teens continually feel that they are damned if they do and damned if they don't. For example, your daughter slams the door in your face, but when she comes out 45 minutes later, she is angry that you didn't come in and try to talk with her. By its very nature, adolescence sets parents (and kids!) up to make mistakes. It happens. When it does, it's okay. We have both made numerous mistakes with our own children; in fact, we consider ourselves to be true experts when it comes to mistakes. Mistakes help you learn, as long as you can keep your sense of humor and remain emotionally available to your teen. Remember, this is an opportunity to model for them how to handle their own mistakes.

The Role of Conflict and The Family Hierarchy

Nobody likes the constant parent-child bickering and arguing that is part of adolescence. But you can't stop it, and it's probably not a good idea to try. Believe it or not, conflict is a healthy and necessary part of adolescent development, part of the process of separation between a teen and his or her parent. The parent should not view this as rejection, but rather as the teen's assertion of his own independence and individuality (even if this assertion is not particularly graceful, articulate, or well coordinated). You can, however, mitigate the types of conflicts you have and teach your teen how to handle conflict appropriately.

By modeling appropriate ways to handle conflict, you not only teach your teen a valuable developmental skill, but you underscore your own role as the parent, the top of the family hierarchy. Parents need to be parents first and friends second. Your teen needs to know that you are ultimately in charge, and that you are strong enough to set boundaries and enforce them. Maintaining a healthy and appropriate family hierarchy is essential to helping your teen learn how to assert herself, to navigate the numerous pitfalls of adolescence, and ultimately to separate and mature into an independent responsible adult.

Process versus Content

Ultimately, this book focuses on process rather than on content, on *how* you do and say things versus *what* you actually do or say. To tell the truth, how you interact with teens—making them feel safe and secure, allowing them to learn for themselves and showing them respect—is often infinitely more important than many of the individual topics you discuss: who is right or wrong, what clothes your daughter should wear, what car your son should drive, or what status your teen achieves in school. If you get the process right, the content will follow.

It's Only a Phase!

Above all else, keep in mind that adolescence is only a stage, and that it will eventually be over. In this regard, parenting a teen is just like what you have already done in parenting your child through other developmental phases. Remember how the terrible twos felt like they would never end? But you successfully parented your way through that phase, and eventually, it was over. You survived, and so did your son or daughter. Adolescence, too, shall pass.

CHAPTER 2

WHAT IS YOUR PROBLEM?

Adolescent Development

For many parents, one of the most puzzling and frustrating features of adolescent development is its seemingly random nature. Teens' behavior and communication can be unpredictable, even paradoxical, from day to day (or from teen to teen). There is a method to the madness, however. Adolescence is nothing less than the struggle to bridge the gap between the dependency of childhood and the autonomy and interdependency of adulthood. In effect, your teenager is pushing you away while constantly looking back and reaching out for you. Before we address the specific issues that teenagers (and parents) may face during this tumultuous time, it is important to understand that many of these issues are directly or indirectly related to the enormous physical, emotional, and intellectual changes that occur during adolescence.

Biological Changes

Outside

In one sense, the beginning of adolescence is signaled by the onset of puberty, the physical and sexual maturation that young men and women experience at this time. The hormonal and biochemical changes that accompany puberty trigger the abrupt biological and emotional changes that are the hallmark of adolescence.

Adults probably notice these changes first as they occur in the teenager's physical appearance. At about age 11 or 12, girls begin to grow body hair under their arms, on their legs, and in the groin. Their breasts begin to develop and they begin to menstruate. Boys tend to enter puberty slightly later than girls. At 13 or 14 years old, they begin to gain weight, develop body hair (including in the groin and under the arms), experience an increase in penile and testicular size, and their voices begin to deepen. Almost every adult man can recall an embarrassing story about when his voice began to change, which is a polite way of saying when his voice cracked and squeaked at the most inopportune and humiliating moment possible.

Inside

These overt physical changes reflect a host of internal hormonal changes. Generally, hormonal changes in females are tied to mood, feelings and emotions, whereas the hormonal changes in males lead to an increase in physical activity. Thus, these biological changes affect males and females in very different ways. Each set of changes brings with it its own difficulties and challenges for parents.

During puberty, girls begin to produce the hormones estrogen and progesterone. In addition to heightening their senses, increased levels of these hormones also produce emotional instability, mood swings, and irritability. Because these mood swings are, at least in part, hormonally driven, they can appear to be overreactions to simple, everyday situations. (For this reason, some parents feel that adolescent girls are more difficult to raise than adolescent boys.) Also, girls are more verbal than boys. Their speech and language skills may mature up to a full year earlier than boys; they have more neural activity in the speech centers of the brain, and they may use up to five times as many words per week than their male counterparts. This difference is even more pronounced for words and phrases having to do with emotion. Whereas boys say, "I think," girls tend to say, "I feel," and teenage girls may be impulsive and intrusive with their feelings and verbal expression.

Parents can expect their teenage girls to socialize, chat on the phone, and write volumes of notes as they search for emotional outlets and social expression. Although normal and age-appropriate, this social expression can often divert teenage girls from other important activi-ties, such as their academic and family responsibilities. Parents may also begin to see their daughters becoming engaged in verbal conflicts with both peers and teachers.

Parents of adolescent boys are confronted with a somewhat differ-ent set of issues. Young men, at this stage, show a marked increase in the production of the hormone testosterone. Testosterone triggers an increase in red blood cells, which leads to an increase in the body's ability to transport oxygen. Boys' physical endurance improves dra-matically, making them more prone to engaging in physical activities, such as sports. Similarly, increased testosterone levels have been shown to be associated with increased references to physical tasks and activi-ties, and decreased references to emotions. Thus, adolescent boys are driven, biologically to be much more focused on physical actions and behaviors than on feelings, emotions, and other interpersonal factors. Because they are always on the go, and they have an increased energy level but no forethought as to how to expend this energy and how this may affect those around them, some parents feel that teenage boys are more difficult to raise than teenage girls.

Whereas adolescent girls tend to break verbal boundaries, males at this age traditionally break physical ones. In our clinical setting, ado-lescent boys are sometimes brought to us because of an increase in their activity level or impulsive behavior, which may manifest itself in their schoolwork and in their interactions with others. Their parents, justifiably concerned, often ask us if their sons are suffering from at-tention-deficit/hyperactivity disorder (ADHD) or depression, or whether this is just typical adolescent behavior. It can be hard to tell. Some-times psychological testing is needed to tease apart the differences be-tween behaviors that are a part of normal developmental stages or phases, and those that may indicate a specific clinical syndrome.

For example, a pediatrician recently referred Sam, a seventh grade student who was having difficulty in school. According to his teachers, Sam was restless and inattentive in class, would leave his seat and touch, punch, and poke other students, and was preoccupied with other concerns (friends, Nintendo, and so on) during school. These symptoms seemed to imply the possibility of ADHD, which more than likely would mean treatment with stimulant medication. Psychological testing and a thorough social and developmental history indicated that this was not, in fact, a case of ADHD, however. A more likely explanation was that Sam was experiencing hormonal surges, typical for boys his age, that were affecting his behavior and schoolwork. Rather than recommending an evaluation for medication, we made behavioral recommendations, including limiting TV and computer time, and a significant increase in physical activities, such as martial arts, hiking, and team sports. Within a matter of weeks, this increase in physical activities lead to an improvement in Sam's school performance and classroom behavior. Rather than fighting against Sam's natural early adolescent inclinations, we recommended strategies that were consistent with his developmental needs.

At this age, parents may very well see their usually polite and sedate son begin to wrestle with anyone or anything in sight. He may become somewhat oppositional and provoke verbal altercations; he may engage in risk-taking activities; he may even begin to experiment with drugs as a means to satisfy his newfound lust for stimulation, or to calm him down. The industrial revolution and the new technological revolution have removed many of the natural physical activities that males previously used to express themselves, and contemporary society requires a male's emotional development to occur in other, nonphysical ways. Parents of male adolescents need to be aware of the biology that they are fighting against as they socialize their sons into the world of adults, and take care to provide physical outlets to allow their sons to diffuse this increased energy.

Thus, adolescent females find themselves in the midst of a hormonally fueled emotional roller coaster and tend to externalize their feelings. Girls need help in identifying, understanding, and articulating these often confusing and erratic emotions. Males tend to express themselves through their behaviors, while internalizing their feelings and shying away from talking. Boys need help expressing themselves verbally, learning appropriate social interaction.

Interpersonal Changes

Teens' internal biological changes are matched by equally dramatic and powerful external changes. For as much as a teenager develops individually at this age, there is an equally dramatic development and maturity in their interactions with others. These developments affect both peers and parents.

About the time a young adolescent is in middle school, the influences of his or her peers begin to grow in stature and seem to become as powerful, if not more so, than the influence of his or her parents. Teenagers of this age typically begin to isolate themselves from their families, becoming increasingly self-absorbed. They tend to spend more time alone in their rooms, talking on the phone with friends, playing music, video games, and surfing the Internet. Even though they are focused on their friends, interactions with their parents (heaven forbid!) are vital.

A recent television documentary followed a project in Africa that attempted to save a herd of elephants from starvation during a prolonged drought. Because the sheer size of the adult elephants made them too difficult to transport, park officials moved the baby elephants alone to another preserve. These immature elephants appeared to have been successfully relocated and rescued. Several years later, however, officials began to find dead rhinos in the park to which they had transported the young elephants. Only after diligent observation did zoologists discover that the same elephants that had been transplanted because of the drought, had been killing these rhinos. These elephants, now adolescents, appeared to have formed unruly and violent gangs. The park rangers followed the elephants and confirmed that they were taunting and killing the rhinos, attacking villages, and committing other aggressive acts. The park rangers brought in animal trainers to curb these adolescent elephants' behaviors, but to no avail. It was only after they imported adult elephants from neighboring parks that these adolescents begin to become "socialized." After several months of adult instruction and discipline, the killing and rampaging ceased. Just like the herd of elephants, humans (yes, believe it or not, teenagers are still classified as human) need structure and socialization from someone who cares so they can learn to cope with impulses and emotions and successfully enter the greater culture as productive, healthy adults.

Identity and Independence

Think back to your own teenage years. We all have experienced the conflicts that the transition years of adolescence seem to stir. Some teenagers are vocal, restless, or rebellious; others may be quiet and passive. Nevertheless, each teen needs to try out different identities and sometimes push limits. This can be a frightening stage for the adolescent as well as for the parent. Conflicts will sometimes arise as your child pushes the limits towards more independence or experiments with new identities. This pushing and pulling strains the parent-child relationship during what is arguably the most profound developmental phase of our children.

As parents, we all clearly have expectations for our children and opinions about who they are and how they should turn out. There is no argument that your influence is both significant and essential. It is vital that you realize, however, that it is up to teens to become independent and become comfortable with themselves. Your control and structure must give way to their self-reliance and sense of identity. This is the parents' struggle and conflict.

The need to affiliate with peers is essential to an adolescent's transition from childhood into adulthood. In order to form and crystallize their identity and to separate from their dependence upon their parents, they must explore, develop and experiment with their own unique abilities and desires. To be successful, they eventually must socialize into a specific culture, which they will adopt as their own. This process starts in adolescence and continues until they have more completely established their own independence and have accepted and internalized the norms and values of the culture. This helps to explain why teenagers are so susceptible to trends, cliques, cults, and gangs. They are seeking affiliations and other sources of interpersonal and emotional support that allow them to assert their independence from their families. They use these affiliations as a crucible in which they are to explore and experiment with their sense of who they are and who they would like to become. It seems paradoxical that teenagers, who fight tooth and nail for their independence from their parents, often feel very dependent upon their friends, respond well to highly structured contexts such as the military, and seek out athletic teams or clubs that require conformity to very specific, group-oriented guidelines.

Alex arrived into our office with nose piercings, dyed hair, and Salvation Army black clothing. His parents were divorced and at odds with each other's parenting. His father was furious and frustrated with his son's attitude and attire. His mother was concerned about Alex's emotional state and his distance from his family. His grades were good, but he was not as industrious as he had been previously. His peer group was close but not particularly communicative to adults. We began individual therapy, and Alex opened up readily about feeling caught between his parents. He also said his friends were the only ones he could open up to, that they understood and accepted him, listened to him, and did not judge him. Several of his friends dressed and looked similar to Alex, as though this was their uniform. Black clothing, piercings, and tattoos all symbolize identity and rebellion against traditional appearance. It was important that we address Alex's anger and alienation in therapy, rather than his clothing and piercings. Alex's relationships with both his parents began to improve as the parents each realized the pressure they were putting on him, and his clothes and appearance began to become more traditional.

Many good parents have trouble with their adolescent's identity formation. We often feel that our children should be like us. That's only natural; it's evolutionary. The temptation for parents is to become over-controlling rather than recognizing their teenagers' differences. Instead, you must learn to recognize that your children are separate from you and that their self-esteem and inner strength are bolstered by their developing sense of independence and identity.

It is important that parents and other significant adult figures continue to remain involved and to provide guidance and structure to teens. The teenagers that come to our office privately communicate their need for adult involvement, despite their public statements to the contrary. All teens need lots of guidance and attention from their parents and other important adults in their lives. We cannot overstate this. It doesn't matter that your teens say that they don't even want to be seen in public with you. They need you now.

SECTION TWO

Basic Survival Skills

CHAPTER 3

OVERWHELMED AND OUTGUNNED

The Role of the Parent

When parents come into our office, their questions about their son or daughter range from "why won't she listen?" to "when should we...?" to "Here, you take him, give him back when he is fixed!" Our responses are usually twofold. In addition to talking about the individual differences that make each family unique, we usually spend some time discussing various parenting strategies and styles. This framework helps to provide (or hopefully, more accurately, helps parents to develop for themselves) a "big-picture" view of what goes on in families and what the role of the parent should be. This chapter will help you develop specific strategies and to answer certain questions that arise when parenting an adolescent.

Take Care of Yourself First

What?

When parents ask the types of questions above, what they are usually *really* asking is, "What can we (or should we) do for our teenager?" This is a natural, often noble sentiment. It shows that parents are putting their child first and demonstrates their devotion to their son or daughter. What many parents overlook, however, is what they can do for themselves and each other. Parents' abilities to take care of themselves and support one another are the foundation on which all other parenting responsibilities are built. Parents need to make caring for themselves a priority—not necessarily *the* priority in all cases—but a priority nonetheless.

Now, beginning with a focus on parents may feel like a digression, as though this is nothing more than a prelude to the *real* job of a parent. Some parents may think, "Help myself first? How selfish could I be?" Nothing could be further from the truth. If you do not take care of yourself, you cannot be fully available to your children. Consider the standard pre-takeoff speech on an airplane. After you are seated and are comfortably reading a magazine, a flight attendant inevitably interrupts your reading to tell you some vital information before the plane takes off. He or she dutifully informs you of where the emergency exits and lavatories are located, teaches you how to buckle and unbuckle your seat belt, and tells you that in the event of an emergency loss of cabin pressure, an oxygen mask will drop down in front of you. In this scenario, you are to put the mask over your nose and mouth and breathe normally. If you are traveling with a young child or someone who needs your assistance, your flight attendant continues, you are to put on your own oxygen mask first before helping that person. While it may seem selfish at first, these instructions make sense, and have probably saved many lives. In such an emergency, if you were to pass out while helping someone else, you would both be in danger. Most adults understand this concept when it comes to something concrete, like an oxygen mask on an airplane. But applying the same principles to feelings and emotional support is harder to accept, and even more difficult to put into practice. So how do you take care of yourself as a parent?

Co-Parenting: Spouses Supporting Each Other

Your best source of support as a parent is your spouse. A spouse's support is a vital and often necessary component of avoiding burnout and feeling like an effective parent. Your spouse, more than any other person, can see things from your point of view: he or she knows the issues, pressures, and tensions of your household, your frustrations and concerns. (If this is not the case, then this may be an area of your marriage that is worth examining.)

Your spouse's most critical role may not be helping you come up with a strategy to handle a given situation, although this type of support is helpful, or providing a respite from taking care of the kids, although this can feel like a lifesaver, too. Rather, you may help one another best simply by providing emotional and moral support, acknowledging what each of you is trying to accomplish as a parent, how difficult it is, or how hard you are each working.

Perhaps most importantly, spouses can let each other know that regardless of the outcome, they are doing the right thing. Parenting is like nothing else. Most of us have gone through our lives learning that if we do the right thing and make the right decisions, we will be successful. It was true in school, true when we started working, and even, for the most part, true in relationships. Unfortunately, however, this is not the case when it comes to parenting. You can be the perfect parent, and still have your children (particularly teenagers) test the limits, misbehave, and end up arguing with you or being grounded for a week. Although doing the right thing as a parent will lead to success in the long run, it will *not* necessarily lead to success, or even help you to avoid conflict, in the short run. This is probably not a surprise to anyone who has been a parent for any length of time, but it is still vitally important to receive feedback, praise, and simple acknowledgment from your husband or wife on a regular basis, and to give it in return. This is the best way for parents to maintain their self-esteem, cope with frustration, and refrain from beating themselves up by constantly second-guessing their actions.

Being supportive, however, is not nearly as easy as it sounds. Genuinely supporting your husband or wife, not just paying lip service to this idea, requires that both parents really trust each other. It is impossible to co-parent, to work together as a team, without trusting each other. We all make fewer mistakes when we feel that our partner and teammate believes that we will do the right thing and that whatever mistakes we make will be exceptions to the rule and nothing more.

But how do you handle it when you honestly disagree with your spouse? Again, the answer comes back to trust. Parents must be confident that their overall goals and philosophies about child rearing are similar. It is often easier to compromise on a small, specific issue just for the sake of supporting your husband or wife, or even to just keep the peace, when you feel certain that you are being supported in the larger, overarching issues.

To get to this point of mutual agreement and trust, parents have to communicate—often, honestly, and thoroughly. The real work comes in the form of the long, even repetitive discussions between you and your spouse during which you decide upon your parenting philosophies. *This does not just happen by itself.* Both parents must consciously and purposefully work together on this before issues actually come up with your children. This includes discussions between the parents about curfews, how to discipline, appropriate punishments, and priorities concerning school, homework, and extracurricular activities. Remember when you and your spouse were dating, and you used to have "pillow talk"? Well, this is what pillow talk is now, when you have a teenager. The answers to issues will, and probably should, change from time to time as your adolescent matures. What is important is the process by which you and your spouse address and discuss these issues. If you make a commitment to discuss these types of issues and decide how to handle them before problems develop, it will be possible to take crises in stride when they do occur.

Okay, so what if problems already exist? What if you are already in the throes of it? First, take a deep breath and resist the urge to fix it (whatever it is) yesterday. Don't make decisions like it's the bottom of the ninth—no matter what the score is, it is only the fourth inning. Despite how it feels, there is plenty of time to help your teen develop into a happy, successful independent adult. So back to the question at hand, what do you do? Tonight, start the discussion with your spouse about getting on the same page as parents, developing trust, and supporting each other. In addition, as part of this discussion, talk about the immediate issues at hand that have to do with your kids (school, discipline, chores, etc.). It may feel easier to tackle these issues in the context of this larger discussion about co-parenting, even on the first night. Check in with each other about the issues in your co-parenting relationship on a regular basis. Keep talking—it's the only way you'll establish the type of communication and support that you're looking for. It probably won't change all at once, but it is a start.

This process of parents working together, respectfully disagreeing, and ultimately compromising, is more than just a sound strategy for coping with the pressures of raising an adolescent. Its greatest benefit is what it models to the teenager about relationships and how people interact with each other. Teens are fervently concerned about relation-ships and how they work; they are primed to learn about how people interact and relate to each other. Thus, your actions as parents need to be effective now, but they also need to be something you will feel com-fortable with having your children imitate and repeat in the future.

Co-parenting in this style also helps to counteract one of your adolescent's most effective means of causing havoc and chaos in your home: splitting the parents. *Splitting* refers to a teen's ability to play one parent against the other. Teens are adept at driving a wedge between their parents. For example, your teen may react to you and your spouse as though you have been assigned roles, such as the "good" parent and the "bad" parent. Though subtle, this can be extremely pow-erful and effective in cracking parents' unified front. Because of the acute knowledge they have about their families, and the immediate gratification they achieve through splitting their parents, this is one of the easiest methods for teens to achieve the natural goal of asserting themselves and their control over their surroundings. Unfortunately, splitting is inevitably a self-defeating process. It is a quick fix, as op-posed to more mature methods of asserting yourself, to say nothing of the negative effects it has on parents. But if you and your spouse com-municate about and are united as a team in your parenting approach, you will be more apt to recognize when your teen is trying to split you, and you'll both be less likely to play into it.

Avoiding Burnout

So now we have discussed parents' need to work together and why this is important. But actually putting this into practice is much, much more difficult. How do you do all of this, and keep on doing all of this for weeks, months, even years at a time? How do you avoid burning out as a parent? Once again, the answer lies in feeling supported by your spouse, and in sometimes putting yourself first.

Give yourself breaks, vacations, and rewards, just like you do for your children. Parents often come into our office exhausted, frus-trated, and overwhelmed. But this is not, they tell us, why they are seek-ing treatment. Their concern is their teenager. At the beginning, one of our most common suggestions to parents is to take some time for themselves—whether it's by going out to dinner or going away for the weekend—and just relax and speak in complete sentences again. It is surprising how effective this simple, even rudimentary intervention can be.

Another helpful strategy for avoiding burnout is to think back to the time before you were a parent. Remember what you looked forward to about being a parent, what excited you about the prospect of having a child or children. Did you want to teach your son or daughter how to cook, introduce them to art, or take them to a baseball game? These are things you *enjoy* about being a parent, the rewards for the hard work you put in the rest of the time. You deserve these rewards, and there is nothing wrong with sometimes doing some of these activities with your son or daughter simply because you want to. Frequently, spending an afternoon with your teenager just having fun can be relaxing and energizing and help you regain some of your excitement about parenting.

Remind yourself and your spouse that this is only a phase, (only a phase, only a phase, only a phase). This is similar to when your teenager was a newborn, before he or she could sleep through the night. You probably wondered, "Is this what life is going to be like forever? Will it *ever* get any better?" At times, it probably felt like it would never end, and then, miraculously, all of a sudden, it did. Likewise, adolescence will someday end, and your relationship with your son or daughter will most likely improve. Parents' marital satisfaction hits an all-time low during their children's adolescence. Stress hits an all-time high, and it is not uncommon to feel discouraged, disappointed, and disillusioned. But, eventually, it will be over, and you'll get your child back again. When teens become young adults, they usually do not retain their adolescent characteristics of moodiness, irritability, and defiance.

Support for Single Parents

Thus far, everything we have discussed refers to two parents working together as a team. This is certainly the easiest way to parent, but for many families, this is simply not the reality. Although single parents have many additional obstacles to surmount in parenting—and less time to do so—it is perhaps even more important for single parents to make themselves a priority than it is for married parents. When it comes to taking care of themselves, certain issues are especially crucial for single parents—including developing strategies for time management, finding ways to take breaks and avoid burnout, and most importantly, developing a support system. It is vital that single parents get themselves some emotional backup. Parents can receive support from many people in their lives besides a partner: for example, the children's grandparents, a sibling, or a close friend can all be sources of support. For a fuller discussion on parenting for single mothers and fathers, refer to Chapter 9.

Parental Roles

Once parents have met their own needs, they are prepared to into parent their teenager more effectively. Each family has its own unique set of dynamics, and a parent's role in one household may be very different from that of another. Despite these individual differences, however, we have found some common threads from one family to the next. For most families, we conceptualize parenting as consisting of three major roles: the safety net, the bench press/weight training machine, and the teacher.

The Safety Net

Most parents are all too familiar with this role. This is the one that makes you say "no." (In fact, you may feel that that's all you do some days.) This role is much more, however. Parents should not only be there to rescue their teens and pick up the pieces when things go wrong, but also to help set limits and guidelines to help prevent things from going wrong in the first place. To carry the metaphor further, parents are not only safety nets, but they are also the ones who check to make sure the trapeze is hung correctly, so the safety net—hopefully—will not be necessary. Despite the fact that we all know that setting limits is one of a parent's main jobs, it is sometimes difficult to do, and it's rarely appreciated, at least not while your child is still an adolescent. Here, then is a brief pep talk to remind you that you're headed down the right path.

Parents set the limits and provide structure for their children, whether they are 6 or 16. It is okay if your teens disagree with you when you do this. You have a different perspective than any teenager could possibly have, and you can't realistically expect them to always see things from your point of view. Some of your decisions may be unpopular, but you need to make these decisions (about safety, school, curfew, and so on) based upon *your* comfort level, not theirs. You are not doing this blindly. Now, you do have the responsibility to listen to your teen and try to understand their point of view. Sometimes your teen may have very good, legitimate points; nevertheless, you do *not* have the obligation to agree with them. When you do disagree with your teen, you have both the privilege and the responsibility to make the final decision in terms of setting a limit. Families are not democracies, but dictatorships—benevolent dictatorships, but dictatorships nonetheless.

We mentioned that it is both a privilege and a responsibility to say no to your teen. Usually, you are doing teenagers a favor by not shifting this responsibility to them. For example, many school and parent groups that deal with teenage drinking suggest that parents who set firm limits and check up on their children provide an "out" for teens, or a way for them to save face with their friends. In these cases, teens no longer have the responsibility of deciding whether or not to drink— they can just blame it on their parents. By the time they become adults, our teens need to be able to take responsibility for making difficult decisions on their own. Until then, it is helpful and appropriate to allow them to shift some of this responsibility onto us.

The Bench Press/Weight Training Machine

As a rule, when parents bring their teen into our office, they are concerned about their son or daughter and genuinely want to resolve all the issues at hand. As treatment progresses, however, we often find out that what parents are really asking is, "How can we avoid the conflict?" Of course they want to avoid tension, fighting, bickering, and squabbling. These things are unpleasant. Nobody in their right mind would look forward to arguing with a person whom they love. Unfortunately, however, this type of conflict should not, and usually cannot, be avoided totally. What we can and should change is how these conflicts are handled. Although painful, parent-teen conflict is also healthy and important, when kept within certain parameters.

As we discuss parents' roles during adolescence, it is sometimes helpful to keep in mind the teenager's role at this time. During adolescence, teenagers are undergoing the transition from childhood to adulthood. It would be great if teenagers could simply change gears and shift from the old relationships they had with us as children to new ways of relating to us as adults. This is not how it works, unfortunately. Teenagers are not slowly shifting from relating to others as children to relating to others as adults. They are *replacing* one way of relating with another. They are destroying their childhood relationships, ripping apart their old relationship with you (sometimes it may feel as though they are ripping *you* apart!). They do this so that they are then able to form new, more adult relationships. To learn how to be adults, teens need to assert their authority, autonomy, and individuality. They need to practice through trial and error. Young felines, from household kittens to lion cubs, learn to assert themselves and to figure out their abilities and their place in their social structure, by "play" wrestling and fighting. In various species of elk and ram, the young practice the skills they will need as adults by literally butting heads with other elk and rams. Humans are no different. To become adults, our teenagers must assert themselves, testing and refining their own autonomy and confidence.

When viewed in this context, the parent's role in raising an adolescent now starts to make sense. Think of yourself as an emotional bench press or weight training machine. Parents are the tools that teens use to develop, strengthen, and flex their emotional muscles—their confidence and assertiveness. Like physical muscles, these emotional muscles need to be tested constantly to become stronger—a teenager cannot develop these strengths by pushing against his parents only once or twice. It is a process that has value only when repeated. So teens practice for adulthood by pushing against us, their parents. They learn how to assert themselves, they become stronger, more confident, and less dependent upon us, all by pushing against us. And they push against us because we have always been the instruments of their development. As parents, our job is to keep this conflict and tension at a safe and appropriate level. We provide a safe forum in which teens can assert themselves and where they can win or lose without an inordinate amount of risk. At some level, our teens know that this is our role. This is one reason why when they argue with us, it drives us crazy, but it usually seems okay to them.

This process is vitally important. Although the process itself can be quite painful for the parent, when it is not allowed to take place and unfold to its natural conclusion (a mature, healthy adult relationship between parent and adult child) it can be quite painful for the adolescent, now and later in life. For example, Scott was a 26-year-old professional who came to this office because of problems he was having with his parents. He felt that they were being bossy, intrusive, and suffocating. They did not approve of Scott's wife, which put an enormous strain on Scott's marriage. Although his wife kept pushing him to "do something about them," Scott said that he felt intimidated by them, particularly his father, and didn't know what to do. He wanted to be supportive of his wife and to handle them, but he still wanted to have a relationship with his parents. As he discussed these factors in therapy, it became clear that the central issue was his anger at his parents, and his inability to express it. It turned out that he was not so much intimidated by his parents as he was somewhat afraid of his own anger towards them. Family members always avoided conflict in his household, and he never had the opportunity to openly express anger at his parents and to push against them while he was growing up. Now, as an adult, he was still struggling to learn how to separate in this sense from his parents, and to become comfortable with expressing his own anger and assertiveness. When he did learn how to do this, Scott found himself becoming more confident and appropriately assertive in other areas of his life as well.

Thus, conflict between adolescents and their parents is not all bad. It is a necessary and normal part of development. It is tempting to avoid it—as we said, you would be a fool to not want to try—but some conflict is inevitable. Resolving it does not mean preventing these conflicts from coming to the surface. Rather, it means going through the whole process of listening, compromising, arguing, coming to an understanding and working through it.

Sometimes it is helpful to focus on the *process* of your conflict with your teen rather than on the its *content*. *How* our teens say what they say and do what they do is often more important than *what* they actually say or do. If conflict is inevitable, focus on how to deal with it, and resolve it—in effect, how they assert themselves, rather than just on who was right or wrong. We'll discuss this issue of process versus content more in the next chapter.

The Teacher

The final role of the parent is to teach and guide our teenagers. In effect, when we parent our teenagers, we are helping to train them to be adults themselves. Further, we are helping to teach them how to interact with others and how to understand and cope with their emotions. We do this not just with the actual skills we teach them, nor with the rules or structure that we use to guide them. The most powerful and effective method of teaching our teens is using ourselves to model actions, reactions, priorities and attitudes for them. Teenagers often tell us that they feel like they are always being watched, that they are put under a microscope. They don't realize it, but parents have them beat by a mile. Teens meticulously observe our every tiny action, every phrase uttered, and they remember everything. Think back to when your teen was 3, and she accidentally heard you curse or say a colorful phrase. Remember how she would almost immediately start to repeat that word or phrase (despite your best efforts to the contrary) because you used it? Things are no different now. How many times have you corrected your child for doing or saying something, only to have him shoot back, "But that's what Mom does!" or "How come Dad can do that and I can't?"

Although this puts a lot of pressure on parents, it also provides us with a wonderful opportunity. People in general, and especially children and teenagers, have a way of making us feel the way they feel. More than simply making us understand and sympathize with their feelings, they actually induce some of the same emotions and frustrations that they are experiencing. This is one reason teens can make you so angry and upset. That is how they are feeling, and they elicit these same feelings in us. This can often be confusing for parents, who find themselves thinking, "Why do I let him get to me like this?" but it is also an opportunity to demonstrate to your teenager how to deal with difficult, seemingly overwhelming emotions, how to handle things responsibly, and how to discuss and address problems despite your anger. They allow us to go first and to show them the way. If we are successful, they just might follow. We discuss more on this in Chapter 8.

Everything that you teach and demonstrate to your adolescent occurs in the context of your relationship with your teenager. Some of the most effective parenting occurs when you don't even realize you are parenting. Hang out with your teenager. Don't just talk with her when you need to have a serious discussion. What is important is that you are willing to spend time with your kid, and not just on your terms. You will be demonstrating that you care, that you are listening to her and what is going on in her life. *What* you do is far less important than the fact that you are trying to do something, anything—including fumbling all over yourself—to show your teen that you are actively trying to develop a connection with her.

One parent came into our office telling us about his son's disrespectful and oppositional behavior. This parent had dutifully tried to discuss these problems with his son, but somehow, these discussions always escalated into fights, and the problems only became worse. We suggested trying a different tack. Even with the best of intentions, too much of this father's time was spent focusing on his problems with his son. To counteract this, we suggested that the father take his son out for dinner once each week for several weeks. We specifically told them not to discuss anything serious or substantive during these meals. They took our suggestion, and as a result, the two became closer. Nothing was magically resolved. Neither experienced a psychological breakthrough or a moment of epiphany. These dinners will never inspire a screenplay. But their comfort, trust, and communication with each other improved, despite the fact that neither had realized that it needed improvement, and when problems occurred (and they still did), they were easier to address.

Most parents know this, and probably do it more than they realize. Unfortunately, this stance is often confused with being inconsistent. Parents have asked us, "How can you go from being their parent one minute to trying to be their friend the next? Shouldn't you be consistent and stay in the role of parent?" Getting to know your kids and their interests, spending time with them without acting like an authority figure, is certainly consistent with being a parent. Inconsistency does not simply mean doing different things and reacting in different ways. Rather, being an inconsistent parent means that you are sending contradicting messages, and your son or daughter does not know what to expect from you or what you expect from them. If the situation calls for you to take on the role of an authority figure and you do not respond accordingly, then you are being inconsistent. Relating to your teen on occasion as something other than an authority shows that you are confident and comfortable enough in yourself to be flexible—and you are flexible, not inconsistent, when you have the ability to resume your other, more structured roles as a parent when needed. This gives your adolescent the same confidence in you and lets him or her know what to expect from you.

Find the Balance

The issue is not that you as a parent must choose one of these modes, safety net, bench press, or teacher. In fact, you probably shift between these roles effortlessly several times a day. The overall goal is for you to find the right balance of all three of these roles. All three roles are healthy, helpful and appropriate at different times, and the best balance of the three will be different for different teens at different times. As always, when the issue is striking the right balance, it may be easier not to try to get the balance exactly right. Rather, aim to make an equal number of mistakes in all directions. In the long run, you'll find that this helps you delineate a pretty good path.

CHAPTER 4

WHATEVER!

Communication and Trust

Your communication with your teenager is the basis of your relationship with her, and is therefore a powerful resource for parenting, teaching, and shaping your child. Like any tool or resource, it makes sense to invest time and effort in developing it and maintaining it.

Whether you are casually chatting, talking seriously, or fighting furiously with your teenager, there are always at least two issues at hand. One is the *content* of what you are discussing, including how his day was, why she was late, what's for dinner, or how he did on his last algebra test. In addition to content, however, the *process* of communication is also important. This process—how to communicate, as opposed to what to communicate—is the subject of this chapter.

Although the most obvious goal of communication is to impart information, there are many other reasons to communicate as well. In fact sharing information is often not even the primary goal in communication. For example, we communicate in order to feel an attachment or connection with others. This is why teens talk with one another for hours, literally, about nothing. Even adults, when they get together with old friends, often rehash the same old topics and conversations that they have had dozens of times before. One of us has had the same conversation about why Willie Mays is a better baseball player than Mickey Mantle with his older brother at least twenty times. The point of the conversation is not to obtain or convey any new information (there is no new information); rather, the safe and familiar context provides a sense of connection.

Parent-teen communication, in particular, has several other functions in addition to information and connection, and many of these functions are conveyed through the process of communicating rather than the content—the "how" rather than the "what." These functions include establishing trust through listening; setting boundaries; modeling healthy communication skills, particularly in the midst of conflict; and highlighting the hierarchy in the family, which actually provides a safety net for teens as they develop and learn to navigate their emotional autonomy from you. Remember, the goal of all this communication is to foster your teenager's independence. Whatever you discuss with her, whenever you interact with her, the subcontext needs to be you, the parents, supporting and helping her develop her own sense of independence and self-reliance.

Strategies for Communicating with Your Teen

Listen Actively

A very good school counselor we worked with used to say that we have two ears and one mouth, and that we as professionals, adults, and parents need to listen twice as much as we speak. Listening is one of the most important communication tools you have to strengthen your relationship with your teenager.

This is not so different at all from a stage of parenting that you've already been through. Remember when your child was about six months old? At this age, it was natural for her to cry, usually at night, when you were on the phone, or during the fourth quarter of a big football game. Think what you did to calm her down. You never tried to reason with her or to discuss things logically with her. No, you simply soothed and comforted her by holding her. Maybe you said "there, there" or sang to her, but you mainly made her feel safe and secure. Often, you may have found that it was more useful to hold and soothe the baby before you began to focus on resolving what ever was distressing her, whether she was hungry, uncomfortable, or tired. A similar technique can be applied to teenagers. Giving a teenager the opportunity to vent without interruption will often help him feel safer and more secure, soothe his overwrought emotions, and make both of you receptive to finding solutions to the problem at hand.

Adam came into a family session very, very angry with his father. "He's an asshole, he doesn't know what he's talking about, he never listens!" Adam's father tried to calm him down by explaining to the therapist, slowly and calmly, what had happened between Adam and him. Every two sentences or so, Adam would interrupt and tell his father that he was wrong, that wasn't what had happened or what Adam had said, this just proved that his father never listened to him. To Adam's father's credit, he remained calm, but he tried to respond to each or Adam's points by disagreeing, giving his opinion, and sometimes by logically proving that Adam was mistaken. He kept wanting Adam to see the truth. This, of course, only made Adam even angrier.

Finally, the therapist intervened to stop this cycle. He told the father that he was not allowed to respond, disagree or even give his opinion, at least not yet. He was only allowed to listen and acknowledge. This was difficult and required some coaching. (One parent in this position once exclaimed, after much trial and error that he didn't know how to acknowledge.) It wasn't until Adam's father was able to do this and Adam had a chance to vent and to feel listened to, that Adam was able to calm down. Then and only then was Adam's father able to discuss the content of what Adam had said, to disagree with him, and to have Adam understand. The father's fatal error was trying to apply logic and reason to an inherently emotional, and therefore illogical and irrational, situation. Once the emotional needs were met (the equivalent of holding, saying "there, there" and soothing a six-month-old), they could then move on to address the logical realities of the situation, and find solutions. The problem for Adam's father was not whether he was right or correct (in this case, he was), but rather one of timing.

As you probably recall from when your child was a baby, this technique only works when you, the parent, feel comfortable and relaxed. Have you ever seen a new father with no experience with babies try to hold his crying infant son or daughter? He is often very stiff and wooden and unsure of himself, and the infant picks up on this and cries harder. This inevitably causes the father to feel more unsure, which, in turn, makes the baby more insecure, leading to even more distress. (This cycle usually continues until the father's mother-in-law takes the baby and calms it down in about three seconds, which *really* makes the father feel insecure.) You cannot provide your teen with a safe space to communicate his or her frustration if you are unsure of yourself as a parent, angry, exhausted, or otherwise unable to give your teen your full attention. You must be able to show him that you are listening. This type of focused listening also puts you in a good position when you want to talk to your teenager later about how he communicates with you and the importance of listening and being polite and respectful.

Set Boundaries

Help your teens establish and maintain boundaries. When we talk about boundaries, we're talking about teenagers and parents alike taking control and ownership of their behaviors, communication, and how they express their emotions without becoming overly involved, overly invested, or overly intrusive into other people's lives. Sometimes there are issues that parents need to discuss that just simply are not the teenager's concern. Similarly, there are aspects of the teenager's life that may not be the parent's concern. Maintaining boundaries not only helps to foster independence for your teenager, but helps to reinforce the hierarchy of the family.

For parents, maintaining boundaries sometimes means allowing your teen to make mistakes, even when you know they're making a mistake, and you have the ability to prevent them from doing so and getting hurt. Sometimes we need to allow teenagers to make their own mistakes so that they can learn from them. For example, Eric's girlfriend cheated on him and they broke up. He was devastated. After about a week, she wanted to get back together. Both Eric and his mother agreed that if he went out with her he would probably be hurt again. His mother tried to talk him out of it to protect him from getting hurt. But Eric felt that he needed to give their relationship another chance. Even though Eric knew that his mother was probably right, he and his therapist agreed that it should be Eric's decision, even if it turned out that it was the wrong decision and his mother was right. Sometimes it is more helpful to make your own mistakes and get burned than to be protected from making a mistake in the first place.

Model Effective Communication Skills

One crucial function of parent-teen interaction is that it models effective and acceptable methods of communication. Every time parents speak with their children, they are teaching them how to express themselves. If you are short-tempered and quick to snap at your children, then you are teaching them to be short-tempered and quick to anger with others. If you appear to not pay attention to them when they speak, they most likely will appear to not pay attention to you when you speak. And if you avoid discussing difficult topics, then you are teaching them that this is an appropriate strategy.

MISTAKES

As we've mentioned, we can think of few other roles in which an individual is under as much scrutiny as a parent is. Your every action and reaction is watched and critiqued. Of course it's not fair, but this is the way parenting works. Realistically, unless you are endowed with superpowers, you will make mistakes. When you do make a mistake, it is an opportunity to model for your son or daughter how to accept and handle it.

For example, two parents came into our office with a son who was just entering puberty. Their neighbors had gone on vacation for a week, and the son was in charge of going over to their house to feed their dog. During this time, the mother found a set of girl's underwear in the son's drawer. He had obviously "borrowed" it from their neighbor's teenage daughter and was very curious and aroused by it. He was also incredibly embarrassed. Despite being caught red-handed, he would not admit what he had done. Even when he was told that his feelings were natural, that this was nothing to be ashamed of, and that if he told the truth he would receive a lighter punishment, the son refused to take responsibility for his actions. While discussing this in our office and becoming very frustrated, the parents began talking about how to handle this with their neighbors. Without much debate, they both agreed that if the neighbors asked any questions or accused their son of anything, they would deny it. It wasn't until they noticed their own hypocrisy that they decided, in front of their son, they too would tell the truth and take responsibility for something very, very embarrassing so that their son was able to do the same. Directly or indirectly, your communication can be a way to show your teenager how to take responsibility for his or her actions and deal with frustration and embarrassment.

CONFLICT

Your communication with your teenager also provides a forum for them to push against you, while you teach them to do so appropriately. As we discussed in the last chapter, it is healthy, even important, for teenagers to have some amount of conflict with their parents. This helps to teach teens how to be confident and assert themselves, and how to successfully and appropriately navigate conflict and disagreements. Most of us are not born with these skills, but develop them through practice. As a parent, part of your job is to allow your child the space and opportunity to hone these abilities in a safe and secure environment. It's important that you stand up to your teenager, to not try to sidestep or avoid these conflicts. Your teenager needs you to be his emotional bench press—you have to be strong enough for him to push against. But you have to be able to handle this conflict well to teach him to do the same: you need to able to calm yourself down, help calm your teenager down, and show him how to resolve conflicts rather than trying to win them. By the same token, if you try to avoid conflict, you're teaching him to avoid conflict himself for the rest of his life.

When conflicts do arise, and they will (often when you've had very little sleep), it's helpful to keep in mind the distinctions among *disagreeing*, *arguing*, and *fighting*. We once asked a teenage therapy group of ours to define these terms. After about a half-hour, they came up with definitions better than anything we could ever have come up with on our own. According to these teenagers, *disagreeing* is when parents and teenagers simply look at something differently and they don't agree on it. *Arguing* is when parents and teenagers disagree, and they're still listening to each other, but they're not being polite or respectful. *Fighting* is when they're disagreeing, but they're not listening or being respectful. Notice how these characteristics are not simply about what the teenager is doing to the parent, but also what the parent is doing to the teenager. All communication is two-directional.

Emphasize the Positive

Many of us are much more likely to point out when our kids make mistakes or frustrate us than to praise their good behavior, especially when we are in a period of high conflict in our relationship with them. If you want your teenager to continue to do what's expected of her, by far the best way to encourage this is to acknowledge and reinforce it. Set a goal for yourself of saying two to three times as many positive things as negative things to your son or daughter. If your relationship with your teen is very tense, this may be a real struggle. If need be, you can actually set your child up to succeed so that you have the opportunity to point out something positive.

Dr. Gold used to work in a group home. One teenager there was having a very rough time and was constantly butting heads with the staff. Dr. Gold decided that he would try to find something positive to say about him the next day if it killed him. Sure enough, it almost did. By about four o'clock, despite his best efforts, Dr. Gold could not find anything positive to say to this poor kid. So Dr. Gold called him into the kitchen and told him that he wanted to speak with him. Before he started, Dr. Gold said, "Hey Johnny, could you hand me that glass over there? I need a drink." Johnny turned around and handed him the glass. Dr. Gold made a big deal out of this: he thanked him and told him that he really appreciated Johnny handing him that glass the first time he asked, without any backtalk, and that Dr. Gold was proud of him. Johnny looked at him and said, "You know, you did that on purpose." Dr. Gold responded, "Yes, I did," and he explained that he thought it was important to show Johnny that the staff noticed the positive things he did as well as the negatives. They had a great conversation and, for the short term, they found that there were significantly more positives to acknowledge and to talk about.

One way to emphasize the positive for teenagers is to communicate to them that there's a distinction between who they are and what they do. Many parents who did this quite automatically when their children were 2, 3, and 4 years old, (by saying, for example, "I love you, but I don't like what you did just then") forget to emphasize this distinction as their children reach adolescence. Their behaviors can be good or bad, and it should be okay (in fact, it is a parent's duty) to say whether you agree or disagree with these behaviors. You need to show your teenager that you feel that they themselves are good, however, and that you unconditionally love and accept who they are, even when you dislike their behavior.

Similarly, there's a distinction between feelings and behaviors. When you were growing up, didn't you hate it when someone would tell you not to feel a certain way? "Don't be afraid," "don't be sad," "don't get angry." Most of us can't control the actual feelings that we experience. It's always okay to have feelings, and this certainly includes anger. What may or may not be acceptable, however, are how we express these feelings in behaviors. By communicating to your teenager that you love and value him and accept his feelings, despite his actions, you are establishing trust, and ideally, creating a secure space for your teen to evaluate and change his behavior.

Reinforce the Family Hierarchy

Your communication with your teenagers helps to highlight and support the hierarchy in the family. As we have discussed, families are not democracies, but are actually structured with a very clear hierarchy. Parents are in charge; children, teenagers, grandparents, aunts, and uncles are not. But the hierarchy in a family does not simply mean that parents are in charge and that they have all the privileges. Rather, it means that parents have the all the *responsibility* for making decisions. By taking responsibility, parents serve as a safety net for teens.

For example, part of the parent's hierarchical role is the responsibility to help change things when they do not go well. When they fight, parents and teenagers often have the same frustrations, fears, and insecurities. In these situations, it is very easy for parents to fall into the mindset of, "I'll apologize once she apologizes," or, "I'll listen after he listens," or, "I'll respect her once she respects me." Despite how it feels in these situations, you are the parent, and it's very important that you take responsibility by being the one to apologize first, listen first, or show respect first. This helps teach your teenager how to handle these types of situations. Your communication with your teenager must reflect the fact that you take responsibility for anything and everything in the family. This places the power and the strength in the family clearly with you, the parent, and you will then be able to use this strength to be a resource and to help your teenager be more independent as he or she matures into adulthood.

Communication Styles

We'd like to take you through an activity we often use in seminars to illustrate the differences among three different styles of parenting, or in effect, three different patterns of communication. Imagine that you are together in a group of parents, and as a group, you rotate through three separate stations. At each station, there is a facilitator to provide instruction to build something with whatever materials are there at that station.

At the first station, the facilitator is sitting on a chair reading a magazine, paying very little attention to you. Eventually, one of the parents in the group asks the facilitator, "What should we do?" The facilitator simply looks at her magazine and says, "It doesn't matter. Do whatever you like." Even if the group persists, the facilitator refuses to answer your question and continues reading the magazine. Sometimes you build something at this station, sometimes you don't.

At the second station, the facilitator is a little bit more active. He takes suggestions from the group about what you should build and how you should build it. He helps to organize the group about who should do what. This facilitator also makes a point of incorporating new ideas and other people's perspectives into the project as you go along.

The third group is a little bit different. This facilitator is even more direct. He not only tells you what to do, but also tells you where to sit, how to sit, and what to say. He'll give you instructions such as, "Pick up the blue block. No, use these two fingers. Pick up the blue block like this. Turn it 90 degrees and place it on the red block." This facilitator does not accept input from the group, nor does he tolerate suggestions or interruptions.

At the end of the exercise, the group discusses which station produced the best results, which produced the worst results; which stations had the best and worst communication between facilitator and group members; which had the best and worst communication among group members; which station was the most enjoyable, and which station was the least enjoyable. For the most part, group members give the answers you'd expect. Most of them like station number two, and report that this one gives the best results. Groups typically report the most negative feelings about station number three.

Now comes the trick question. Which is the style of parenting that illustrates the best pattern of communication to have with your teenagers? Most parents who do this exercise choose style number two. Now, style number two has several good qualities, and in many ways, we like this as a good default. Like we said, however, this is a trick question.

The most effective style of parenting and of communication is not any single style illustrated in this exercise. All are good, useful, and important. The best style of parenting is to be able to switch effectively from one style to another, and to make use of all three styles as appropriate when communicating and interacting with your teenager.

For example, if it's a Saturday afternoon and there's nothing on the agenda and no responsibilities that need to be met, it makes sense to use style number one. This style is sometimes called "laissez-faire," and allows teenagers to make decisions for themselves and to take responsibility for their actions and their decisions, within reason. This style is very low on communication. There isn't much give-and-take between parent and child in this style. It's also very low on structure and, when you stop and think about it, very low on nurturing. The parent does not give a lot of support, guidance, or even feedback to the teenager in this style.

Style number two is called "authoritative," and as we said, it is a good default style. An authoritative parenting style, or an authoritative leadership style, provides a good deal of communication. It's also relatively structured. In this style, the parent does offer a good deal of guidance, feedback, reinforcement, and support to the teenager. In addition, an authoritative style helps promote autonomy and independence in teens by encouraging them to be active in making decisions and taking responsibility for their decisions. Finally, an authoritative style provides a fair amount of nurturing.

The last style is called "authoritarian," and it is no coincidence that it sounds very much like number two, the authoritative style. In many regards, these two styles are more similar than they appear on first inspection. An authoritarian style, like number two, emphasizes structure, but it offers substantially less two-way communication. In addition, an authoritarian style does not do much to promote independence and autonomy. Parents who rely on this style too much may be setting their teenagers up to be dependent on them and their decisions, or to be overly reactive and to constantly position themselves in opposition to others' decisions. Finally, an authoritarian style is quite low on nurturance and does not provide a great deal of support. Despite its shortcomings, however, the authoritarian style does have its place. For example, when your children were younger and you were crossing a street with them, you needed them to walk when you told them to walk, stop when you told them to stop, to stand next to you and not two feet to the left, and to do it NOW. For teenagers, it may be necessary and wise to tell them when, where, with whom, and under what circumstances and conditions they may and may not drive. In situations similar to this, you should not apologize for being this directive or authoritarian. It's the correct and safe thing to do.

The best way to be a parent is to not be afraid of any of these three different communication styles, but to find a balance among the three, and to be comfortable switching from one to another as the situation dictates. The parents who come into our office with the greatest difficulties are often those parents who feel constrained to use two or sometimes even only one of these parenting styles, and do not feel comfortable or confident using all three.

Tips for Parents

As with most aspects of parenting, there is more than one correct or healthy way to do things. Although this is certainly true when it comes to communication, the following is a collection of things that we've found that have been helpful to many of the parents with whom we work.

1. To begin, always listen first. There's plenty of time for speaking later. Listening by itself is not enough, however. If you listen, but you don't make them *feel* as though you're listening to them, then you're not fulfilling your end of the bargain.

2. Remember, however, that listening does not mean agreeing. When teenagers ask us to listen to them, they're often asking us to agree with them. Although you need to listen to them and acknowledge what they're saying, you don't necessarily have to agree.

3. Some conflict is healthy, even necessary for kids to learn how to handle such situations. When conflict occurs, as it inevitably will, try to keep the distinctions among disagreeing, arguing, and fighting in mind. Your goal should be to keep conflicts at the level of disagreements or arguments, rather than letting them escalate into fights.

4. When disagreeing or arguing with your teenager, or anybody for that matter, talk about yourself and your feelings rather than making accusations and assumptions about the other person or their feelings. This is often called using "I" statements. There is a difference between saying, "I disagree," versus, "You are wrong." It often comes across as less accusatory, less threatening, and can keep disagreements from escalating into arguments or fights. But no cheating! It's not okay to say, "I feel that you're wrong."

5. Never make assumptions about how or what your teenager is feeling. Rather, ask her what she is feeling and discuss it with her.

6. Remember that we as parents need to admit our mistakes. How you handle the mistake is often much more important than what the mistake actually was. Parents need to model this for teenagers by being honest, taking responsibility for what they've done, and making amends. After all, this is exactly what we want them to do.

7. When discussing your adolescent's friends, (or, more to the point, when arguing with your teenager about his or her friends), don't make it personal. Teenagers are very loyal to their friends. If you start criticizing his friends, you're just opening the door for your teenager to defend his friends and argue with you. Instead, try talking about the behaviors that upset you rather than rather than the friends who display those behaviors. Ask him whether these behaviors, in general, are good or bad, positive or negative, regardless of who's performing them. It's much easier to help your teenager to be objective and to develop some level of insight and perspective this way.

8. Finally, at least once a week, spend some time with your teenager talking, listening, and working on your relationship. Take him out for food, and don't talk about school, or homework, or responsibilities at home. Just talk with him about things that he wants to talk about—friends or girlfriends, television, movies, music, whatever he'd like. Spending this type of casual time is by far is the most important thing you can do to improve and develop your communication with your teenager. And remember, you have two ears and only one mouth.

CHAPTER 5

THE BIG SPLIT

Helping Your Teen Develop Healthy Independence

Despite the fact that we spend a good portion of our children's young lives telling them that they have to listen to us, our goal as parents is to help them get to a point where they can think for themselves, and where we can trust them to do so. To accomplish this goal we must shepherd our children through a successful emancipation and into independence. As our society has become more complex and expectations increase, the age of independence also has increased. It may surprise you to learn that today the average age that both adults and youngsters ascribe to "adulthood" is 26 years old. This age has steadily increased each decade over the last 50 years, so when we think back to our own "coming of age" the expectations are not the same for when we were the equivalent ages. Many factors contribute to this increase, including more education, waiting longer to marry and have a family, smaller families, experimenting with a career choices, etc.

All societies have had their "rites of passage" into adulthood integrated into their culture. Native Americans took their young braves into the wilderness and let them survive the elements and the harshest conditions alone during winter months. Some modern societies have used compulsory public or military services as a right of passage. Americans, in contrast, have primarily relied upon marriage, college experiences, or military service as rites of passage that denote the transition into adulthood.

Today, as our culture changes and becomes more complex and teens need to wait longer and longer for adulthood, our own "rites of passage" have evolved. School trips, nature camps, sleepovers, and weekends or longer periods with relatives, church, or other groups all help our kids experience being on their own and signify steps toward maturity.

Preparing children to successfully complete this separation is a process of balance and knowing your child's needs. Most parents handle this process by following society's norms while emotionally and financially supporting their child's talents as they separate, and many parents become angry, frustrated, fearful, or worried when their youngster stumbles or gets stuck. We've developed some principles that may help with parenting these children into adults.

1. Prepare early. Early on, reassure your child, your spouse, and yourself that it is okay to let a baby cry if his or her physical health is good. Babies do learn how to calm and comfort themselves. Your children do not need your constant attention. It's healthy for your child to go to playgrounds, nursery school, and/ or kindergarten and be outside the family for awhile. Help your child develop relationships with other safe adults. Let the security and safety of your relationship extends toward the safety of other adult relationships. Promote early peer relationships and teach healthy peer interaction. Ingrain this philosophy early in your child's life, and then continue it, in different ways and in different forms throughout adolescence (probably until your child is about age 45).

2. Practice making decisions. For teens, separating from parents into healthy independence involves a comfort level with decisionmaking. This will not happen overnight. You can start early: help your children make decisions by giving them choices. As they progress in age, you can increase the menu of choices they can make. Some of our greatest challenges with teenagers are helping them to learn to make complex and responsible decisions. Parents can overparent their children by making too many decisions for them or not allowing them to experience the consequences of their actions, or

they can underparent by not providing appropriate guidance or the opportunities to discuss their decisionmaking.

Appropriate decisionmaking usually involves emotional awareness. Teaching your son or daughter about emotions and why feelings are important is a vital ingredient of successful decisions. Ask: would a particular decision make him or her happy, guilty, proud of him/herself or ashamed? Strong emotional awareness and emotional intelligence are necessary components of successful decisionmaking and further down the line being a confident, independent adult.

3. Let go with a safety net. Assess your child: What is important to you or your adolescent? What are your child's unique traits and abilities? How can you reinforce and create opportunities to help him succeed? What makes him happy, and what are his passions? When you offer various choices to your child, select options that will most likely produce success for him. In this way, he learns to feel confident, effective, and comfortable in his own abilities. It is not about him being "the best," but about him feeling that he (with his own ingrained characteristics and abilities) is a success.

4. Encourage appropriate risk-taking opportunities. A teenager who has not experienced risk and disappointment may avoid decisions promoting independence. You, the parent, can make it okay to fail or be disappointed. Some of the biggest rewards and greatest gratification can come from taking risks. Trying out for a play or sports team provides examples of risk/reward decisions. Reinforcing these successes and providing emotional support during disappointments is one significant way to help your child build his or her confidence in decisionmaking and therefore learn to take bigger risks. Failure in these situations can be interpreted as building strength, rather than defeat.

When parents and children avoid appropriate risk-taking, parents forge the possibility of becoming fearful, and their children face the prospect of becoming overdependent, which will inhibit emancipation and create dependencies later in life.

5. Economic competence. Like it or not, our society revolves around money. In our clinical practice we see a multitude of teens and young adults who do not have the money management skills to be on their own. Children should start leaning the value of money and money management at very early ages. When parents complain that their young adult child is in constant financial crisis, they often don't have to look very far to find the origin. Often, affluent parents provide a continual supply of money without allowing their child to do without, budget, or save. We recommend that parents start their children off with an allowance, and later with a part-time job. Parents should later encourage their teens to save for larger, more reinforcing items, like a car, that require financial commitment and responsibility, such as paying for (or at least helping pay for) their own gas and insurance.

As adolescents mature, introduce them to debit cards (without overdraft protection). Show them the cost of credit card debt and help guide their budget process. Mistakes and overspending can be valuable early lessons if teens have to accept the consequences. There will be no need for them to budget, sacrifice, or become fiscally responsible if rescue is always just around the corner.

6. Model decisionmaking skills. The most powerful influence we provide to our youngsters is not what we say, it is how we live. By inviting your kids to view your day-to-day life management, you can model the process of successful independence. This does not mean you live perfectly or that your life is problem-free. Quite the contrary, as we discussed in the last chapter, it will only help your teens to see you admit your mistakes and errors, take responsibility for them, and work to solve them. This allows them to see you ask for help and use others for counsel and advice in making important decisions.

Many opportunities are available to allow our teens to view our decisionmaking. They can be involved in school meetings with teachers or counselors. They can watch deliberations at neighborhood organizations, political meetings, and religious organizations or with extended family gatherings. Adults, especially parents, make decisions daily. Our youngsters receive great benefit from viewing and when appropriate, participating in our decisionmaking process.

7. Dealing with fear. Do you remember what you felt before you went out on your own? Although we may have experienced excitement or a sense of adventure, most of us can also remember being fearful about what the future would bring. Rarely do we talk with adults today who had someone to talk to about these fears when they were adolescents themselves. The kids we see now mention that they don't speak of their fears either—unless someone asks them about what they're afraid of when they leave home. Then, suddenly, they are relieved to talk about the many fears they silently contemplate: Will they be able to make it on their own, keep their friends, maintain happiness, be good citizens, or bring pride to their families? Talking about fear is a healthy experience that usually leads to comforting and support from others, reassurance and valuable advice. It helps filter catastrophic thinking and often leads to sorting through tasks and beneficial strategizing. Encourage your teen to share his or her worries, and offer support. Your statements of trust and belief in your children reassure them like nothing else can.

8. Avoid unnecessary rescue. Many parents unknowingly set up a pattern of dependence or a chronic state of insecurity with their teen by intervening too early when a problem occurs. Problems and struggles present an opportunity for your child to grow and gain confidence. When we intervene too quickly we handicap the young person's ability to sort out and solve a situation. The best way to regain confidence and feel pride after an error or downturn in fortunes is to dig your way out of your own mistake.

Instead of fixing your teens' problems, state your belief in their abilities and help them contemplate solutions.

If the parents' anxieties about their teen's self-caused dilemma are motivating them to continually rescue their child, then maybe it is time for the parents to take a look at their own feelings and insecurities. In come cases, it may be helpful for the parents to seek some guidance for themselves. Talk to a school counselor, psychologist, trusted friend, or other parents who have success-fully raised children themselves. They will help you to see that your fears are normal and natural, but that they should not con-trol your decisions nor prevent you from allowing your teens to make and then fix their own mistakes.

9. Step out of the box. The road of separation into adulthood is not always a straight line. Through our years of clinical work, we have become strong advocates of outdoor experience pro-grams, such as Outward Bound and the National Outdoor Lead-ership (NOLS) programs. Programs such as these let young-sters experience and develop self-reliance and independence. Kids also benefit from the emotional and social growth of living with a "new" family group and seeing how they can fit in with and contribute to a larger whole. These experiences can last three days to over three months depending upon the maturity of the youngster and the breadth of experience that is offered.

As your children are faced with lengthier and more complex rites of passage to maturity, these principles should help guide parents and their teens towards healthy separation, and hopefully, successful autonomy in our society. Of course, you will never stop loving, caring, or worrying about your children, particularly when they're in some trouble. You should, however, always contemplate the dangers of bailing them out of that trouble instead of providing an important life opportunity for them to learn and be strengthened. Remember the old adage: "Give a man a fish, feed him for a day. Teach him to fish, feed him for a lifetime."

SECTION THREE

Some Common Hazards You May Encounter

CHAPTER 6

We Don't Need No Education

School, Homework, and Working with the School System

At some point, every parent who comes into our office brings up the issue of school. How is their son or daughter doing in school? How should they be doing? How can they do better? School, they say, is their teenager's job, their responsibility. It is often viewed as a general measure of how the child is doing. The implication is that good kids do well in school, and bad kids don't. In fact, some parents go as far as to say that a good teenager *is* one who does well in school. We can't count the number of times we have heard, "my son is such a good kid, he does so well in school, he could never [drink, smoke, lie, use drugs]!"

School performance is how adults judge teens, and how many teens judge themselves. For some teens, academic performance evolves into a measure of their self-worth or self-efficacy. As psychologists, we feel that academic performance should be valued. It is not the full measure of a person, however, and it should be kept in perspective. Some teenagers simply will not excel academically. This does not mean that they do not have other strengths or that these other strengths should be overlooked or devalued.

Most teenagers don't look at school as an activity that is primarily academic in nature. Ask any group of teenagers what they are thinking about on their way to school, and more often than not, they will say that they are focusing on their friends, the boy sitting next to them in third period or the girl that they are mad at in second period. For teens, school is a social activity, or at the very least, the social aspects comprise a significant part of school. Although parents and other adults may discount or overlook these social factors, they are very powerful, and they affect almost all other aspects of school, from performance in English to a teenager's ability (or willingness and commitment) to focus on homework.

Some teens question the importance of school. Have you ever been asked, "Why do I need to learn algebra? I'm never going to use it anyway!"? Like many of the questions we hear from our teenagers, this one can be extremely intimidating, precisely because it is a very good and very fair question, and one that we may not be entirely sure how to answer. (After all, there is room for disagreement on the issue of the overall importance of algebra to an individual's life.) Your role as a parent, however, is not only to help explain the varying shades of gray, but also to help teach your son or daughter how to do this for themselves in the future.

So how do you explain why teenagers need to go to school to learn algebra and all the state capitals? "Go ask your mother" is one answer. Although this can be quite effective in the short term—about three minutes—take it from us, it doesn't work very well in the long run. We suggest trying one of two other approaches. First, there is the "learning for learning's sake" argument. Education and the accumulation of knowledge may be good and positive in and of itself. This can certainly be true, and can often be a wonderful discussion to have with your teenager. It moves the conversation away from actual behaviors and into the realm of priorities and values. It can lead to the following questions: Who are the people you respect and why do you respect them? What kind of person do you want to be? What kinds of qualities do you want to have? As with most discussions, this should not be one-directional. Parents can and should also answer these questions, both about where they are now and about when they were adolescents. Hearing their parents discuss the change and development that has occurred in their own priorities and values can open teenagers' eyes to the possibility of this (someday) happening to them.

This is the conversation we all would like to have with our kids. But sometimes, they need more immediate and more concrete answers. "Because it's good for you" doesn't always satisfy teens who are looking for a more tangible and specific reason. Try talking with them about going to a job interview. At some point in their lives, all teens will have to apply for a job. In all likelihood, this will be a job that they have never done before, and they will be competing with many, many other applicants for this job. They will need to be able to convince someone that they will be able to learn a new set of skills, to do so effectively and efficiently, and then apply those skills. Moreover, they will have to convince their potential boss that they can be responsible and do what is expected of them, do it on time, work well with others, and be respectful of coworkers and their supervisors. The best way to concretely show this is through their high school and college record because this is exactly what they had to do in school. Specifically, school is learning new skills while interacting and working with others, and it can be looked at as one huge training test that potential employers use to compare, choose, and weed out job applicants.

Now, it is certainly possible to be able to perform well in a job when you did not perform well in school. There may be a reason for not having done well in school, whether it's a learning disability or a lack of motivation or maturity. But then the student/job applicant has to hope that they will have the opportunity to explain this to the one doing the hiring, and that this person will listen, understand, and care. The reality of the situation is that the applicant with a better record will tend to be hired first. It is not always fair, but it's the way it usually works. So, yes, there is a reason to learn algebra: you learn algebra to convince people that you are able to learn other things as well.

What Can Parents Do?

How can you get your teen to do his homework and get better grades? Although there are some strategies that may be helpful, there is no magic pill that will work for every family and every student. (You know the drill; you have heard it before. Insert appropriate disclaimer here.)

As with anything having to do with adolescents, there are two important factors to keep in mind in order to be successful. First, every strategy must be flexible and adaptive over time. Just when you think that you have something figured out, you will probably have to go back to the beginning and start all over again. Be flexible. Secondly, any strategy tends to be more effective if the teenager has a voice in creating and setting the goals and the plan to achieve them.

Most strategies that help with homework and school performance focus on increasing and improving the teen's organization and structure. There are several reasons for this. First of all, helping your teenager to learn how to organize and structure herself provides very useful and concrete skills that will help her for years to come. Secondly, helping her learn structure now will give her the tools she needs *right away* to begin to improve her schoolwork. Notice that we are not focusing specifically on *what* she is learning in her classes, such as French, algebra or history, but on *how* she studies, works and learns. These are skills that are not always formally taught in school, and your teen may need your help to attain them.

Implementing a structure will help prevent teens from making impulsive, emotional, spur-of-the-moment decisions about what they will do when. It is easier to go along with a decision that you have already made to do something, even something unpleasant, than it is to decide to make that decision in the first place. Furthermore, it is often very helpful just to have a plan—any plan—rather than feeling that you are "winging it" and addressing concerns haphazardly as they arise. A plan provides a sense of control and confidence, which in and of itself can be very helpful in improving school performance.

Creating Structure

SPACE

Structure, as it relates to homework, includes a schedule for studying and doing homework, a set, concrete procedure for recording assignments and turning them in, a structured approach to finding appropriate study space and conditions, and the methods your child should use to complete assignments and study for tests. Although these factors may seem self-evident, don't assume they are immediately apparent to your teen.

First of all, discuss where your teen should do his homework. Should he work alone, in his room, at the library, with a friend, and if so, which one? Will he perform his best if he works downstairs at the kitchen table? Different strategies will be effective for different students. In general, however, keep the following guidelines in mind when selecting a study space. First of all, reduce distractions. Distractions include television, little brothers, food, the telephone, e-mail or instant messenger software, and even music. Music is the controversial item on this list. Teenagers often claim that listening to music while they work does not distract them. On the contrary, it helps them to relax and feel comfortable. This may be a very valid point for discussion. As we will discuss below, in addition to minimizing distraction, we also want to provide an optimum level of comfort.

Another general guideline is that it is often preferable for teenagers to do their homework and to study alone. Like the guideline about music, there are several exceptions to this as well. First of all, if a student is resisting doing her work, then it is often preferable to have her study in an area where a parent or other adult can keep an eye on her just to make sure that she is staying on task and doing her work. It is more difficult to go to the "start" menu and play solitaire on the computer when someone is watching you. Secondly, working by yourself can be lonely or boring and potentially very uncomfortable. This can be true for children, teenagers, or adults. And this can potentially interfere with anyone's ability to concentrate and work.

We had one patient who was a very well respected and renowned researcher at a prestigious institute of higher education. He was having a great deal of difficulty with procrastination and not being able to get his work done. It was not a case of not being able to complete his assignments or meet his responsibilities. He was clearly more than capable of doing so. But he couldn't make himself work. He would spend hours sitting and staring at his computer screen, just thinking or trying to distract himself. The answer, for him, was to work with other people around. Rather than working alone in his office, he found that if he went to the library, he was able to work. Similarly, at home, if he worked in the living room or kitchen with his family around, he was able to work.

This is an extension of a very natural and healthy human tendency. For example, a 2-year-old child will typically run all around the house (especially where he is not supposed to go) and then, every 10 minutes or so, run back to his parent. He may want to be held, or simply to play next to you or hug your leg or get underfoot (especially if you are trying to cook or do the dishes), and then, like clockwork, he will be off on his own again. It is almost as though children of this age come back to the parent to get emotionally refueled: they fill up with 10 units of high-octane mommy or daddy, and then they are prepared to go off and face the world alone, at least for the next 10 minutes. This pattern of behaviors is part of what developmental psychologists call attachment theory: the idea that a connection to those who provide us with emotional security just helps us to function better. Healthy attachment has been linked to better per-formance at school or work, better and more stable interpersonal rela-tionships, and a decrease in the prevalence of a number of psychological/ psychiatric disorders, including substance abuse. It can certainly help (some) high school students do their homework better and more efficiently. Thus, in general, it is better to have students do their homework alone in a quiet, distraction-free setting, but for some teenagers, just having some-one else there can help them feel more comfortable and facilitate their ability to concentrate and work.

SCHEDULING AND BREAKS

The next major factor in structuring homework is developing a sched-ule. Set up a consistent, specific, timetable of when homework should be done. It needs to be consistent so that homework is done at a par-ticular time every day, or every weekday, or this particular time every Monday and Wednesday, and at this particular time every Tuesday, Thursday, and Friday. It needs to be more specific than simply "before dinner" or "after dinner"; rather, "homework starts at 4:00." It needs to be flexible enough to allow for the normal, expected and healthy exceptions and events that occur in a teenager's life, however. These may include guitar lessons on Monday, staying after school to work on a project on Tuesday, an extracurricular activity on a Wednesday, or taking an important phone call in order to help out a friend on Thurs-day. All of these activities are good and healthy, and there should be a place for them in addition to (not instead of) homework. Furthermore, a schedule that allows for some measure of flexibility will be signifi-cantly easier to keep and maintain over time.

One of the most important aspects of setting up a schedule is to build in time for breaks. First of all, taking breaks can serve as a reward for working and can help to reinforce this behavior. If you work for 20 minutes, then you can play a video game or have a snack. A quick break provides immediate positive reinforcement. In addition, taking frequent breaks and dividing work up into small, more manageable chunks can make a large project seem less intimidating or imposing. Often, beginning a large project or homework assignment can feel overwhelming. This is true even if the project is something that you have done many, many times before. For example, sometimes when we are writing testing reports as part of our psychology practice, (or a chapter for this book) one or the other of us will sit down, and think, "@#$%! I can't do this." And if we leave it at that, it can be very, very difficulty to get started. We may stare at the computer screen for longer than we care to admit, and not be able to write. But, if we say to ourselves (or each other), "Okay, you're right, you really can't do this. Who are you trying to kid? But even you can write one paragraph for an introduction," we find that we are able to write. It is just easier to think about tackling one small, easily manageable task than a large, complex problem. Large, complex assignments become a series of unimposing smaller tasks.

One potential pitfall of this strategy, however, is that stopping and taking a break every 20, 30, or 40 minutes means that you have to get yourself to begin working again every 20, 30, or 40 minutes. For some students (and psychologists), the hardest part is getting themselves to begin working. Once they get going, they are fine, but making that transition from not working to working can be difficult. Thus, it is important to develop a schedule that provides a balance between taking enough breaks to provide positive reinforcement and to divide their assignments up into small, manageable chunks and of not having too many transition periods that require the student to initiate working in the first place.

One reason that the schedule described above often works is because it is based on the idea of reinforcement, rather than punishment. You are rewarding your teenager with a break after he does a unit of work, instead of punishing or taking away a privilege after he fails to turn in an assignment or after he receives a poor grade. Reinforcement increases the likelihood that a particular behavior will be performed, while punishment decreases the likelihood that a particular behavior will be performed. There is a certainly a place for both. The problem with punishment, however, is that although it helps to decrease certain behaviors, it does not teach or provide other options to replace these unwanted behaviors. If you keep telling your children or teenagers, "don't do that," they probably won't listen to you unless you help them to figure out what they *should* do instead. Thus, any system for improving academic performance should, at least in part, be based on reinforcing positive, desired habits and behaviors.

HOMEWORK LOGS AND OTHER AIDS

In addition to this work schedule, the homework sheet in Appendix A (see p. 64) can also be used to help teach study and organizational skills through positive reinforcement. It is particularly useful for students who have difficulty organizing themselves, and who are in need of a system to help them remember to write down their assignments, remember books, and even turning in the homework that they do complete. Note, however, that this is a starting point. This homework sheet and the structure it defines will almost certainly need to be modified to fit your teenager's needs and the constraints of his or her particular school, and it may even need to be modified from teacher to teacher and from class to class.

The system for this sheet is fairly simple. Each class has its own column. The first row is for the teacher to initial that the homework from the previous day has been turned in. The second row is for the teacher to initial that the student has written down the correct assignment for that evening. The assignment does not have to be recorded on this sheet; in fact, it is often easier to write it in a separate area. (Many teachers, or sometimes even school systems, have specifically prescribed homework logs or agenda books.) Furthermore, in addition to writing down the assignment for each night, it may prove useful for the student to have space in an assignment journal to record any long-term projects and the dates of upcoming tests or quizzes. The third row is for the teacher to initial when the student has written down the materials (textbook, workbook etc.) that the student needs. The fourth line is for the parents to initial when the student shows them his assignments for that evening. The fifth line is for the parents to initial when the student shows them the completed assignment for that evening. The sixth and final line is for the parents to initial when the completed assignment is placed in the homework folder in the student's bookbag. The student should receive one point for each set of initials he receives. These points can then be turned in for some sort of reward or reinforcement. The point is that the students are being reinforced for things that they should already be doing anyway.

The structure that this sheet represents is useful and helpful in several ways. First and foremost, it provides a structure for reinforcing and rewarding positive behaviors. Not only does it provide structure for the student, but it also provides a structure for the parents to sit down every night and focus on some of the positive aspects of their teenager's behavior. In many ways, despite the concrete rewards that teenager earns, praise from his parents is the real reinforcer. Praise from both parents, together, can be a very powerful reinforcer. It is much harder for a teenager to discount praise when there is a second parent echoing the same view. In addition, this structure is not simply a mechanism for reinforcement, but provides communication back and forth between home and school. It lets both parties know exactly when and where problems arise and provides useful information on how to intervene. Finally, notice that for each class, there are three places for teachers to initial and three places for parents to initial. This communicates clearly and concretely to teachers that you are willing to work just as hard as they are at school.

This is not an easy solution by any means, and any or all of the individuals involved may resist it. Students will often resist it because they feel that they are being treated like elementary-school kids and that it is embarrassing to go up to the teacher and to ask for their initials. These criticisms are valid. In fact, in our practice, it is much more common to use a homework sheet like this for students in middle school. If a high school student is having academic difficulty, however, it is certainly not unusual to use a system like this. It requires some effort, but if the teen holds to it, it will work. If she doesn't want to use it, fine. All she has to do is get a certain minimum number of signatures in a specified amount of time, and then she can go back to not using the sheet. But, if she starts missing homework again, then she will have to revert to this system.

Teachers may balk at this too, claiming that they have 30 students and they cannot be expected to keep track of signature sheets for so many students. This too is a valid criticism. It loses some of its bite, however, when the responsibility for getting signatures falls on the student, rather than on the teacher. Certainly by the time a student is in high school, he should have the responsibility for seeking out the teachers instead of the other way around. If a student shows the initiative to try to be organized and to do something to improve his study skills and academic performance, it is not asking too much for the teacher to be supportive of this.

Let us make a few points about rewards and reinforcers. In general, different things motivate different people. Some people like chocolate and will do almost anything in world for a candy bar. Others are weird and do not like chocolate. The only person in the world who knows what will motivate a given person is that person. Therefore, whenever you use any type of reward or reinforcement schedule, the teenager should have a say in what the rewards will be, and the parents should take this into account. The parents have the final decision, however, and they should not necessarily agree with every suggestion their son or daughter makes.

For instance, it is every teenager's right, when using this homework sheet, to request a new car or a trip to the Bahamas as a reward. Under no circumstances should teens be given either of these things simply for doing their homework and getting signatures. But they should be allowed to request certain appropriate rewards that will motivate them. For this system and the rewards to work, the teenager must be successful and earn the reward. Therefore, initially, set the bar relatively low: require relatively few points for your teen to earn the reward. As he becomes better and better at getting initials (and better at completing and turning in homework), raise the expectations and the number of points required in order to earn the reward. You can explain it as a sort of inflation, but it is often helpful to let your teen know beforehand that this is a possibility.

Often, systems like this one work very well in the short term—about one to two weeks—and then they seem to lose their effectiveness. One reason for this is that teens begin to lose interest in the reinforcers. We both really like chocolate, but if you give us candy bars every day in a row for 12 days, we will start to get tired of chocolate and it will lose its effectiveness as a motivator (and we will start to crave donuts instead). Therefore, it is helpful to either rotate the rewards every couple of days, or provide a menu of possible rewards and let your teenager choose. In effect, your teen will then rotate the rewards on his own.

Multiple rewards can makes this type of system very labor-intensive for parents. One way to overcome this is to use cold, hard cash as the reward. Because teenagers can use money to buy any number of other reinforcers that they themselves choose, money is the one reward that does not get old and lose its effectiveness. It has the added extra feature of being one of the few realistic reinforcers that will actually motivate most teenagers. If you do choose to use money as a reward, however, we suggest that the teenager be able to earn, *at most*, just a few dollars each week. Leave room to acknowledge the intrinsic value of education. If you pay too much, it is almost implying that there is no other reason to work at school, that other than this monetary reward, education has no worth. The money should not be the only reason to study.

Remember that you, the parent, are in control of any and all parameters of this system. You should feel free to amend and manipulate these parameters in whatever way you see fit in order to help you focus more on the positive and less on the negatives, and to provide structure, organization, and motivation for your teenager.

Forging a Partnership with the School

When things go wrong, when students get poor grades or fail to work up to their potential or just are not learning, it is very easy to say that the problem is the school. We have heard hundreds of parents complain that the school (or even a particular teacher) is not doing what they are supposed to do, that they are not giving this particular student what they need or what they are entitled to. With the best of intentions, the parents conclude that they need to force the school to do what is right for their son or daughter.

Now, we would never, ever criticize a parent for supporting their child or for advocating for their child's needs. Taking an adversarial stance such as, "I will force you to do what I think is best (or right or fair) for my child," is certainly a fair approach, and it can be useful and appropriate. This is not always the case, however. If a teacher wants to teach a student and is invested in the student, he has a good chance of helping that child to learn. If a teacher either does not want to teach a certain student or he does not feel comfortable or confident in a certain intervention, then he will not be helpful to that student.

For example, Rick was a fifth grade student who was not performing very well academically. Aside from his academic difficulties, however, Rick had a number of very positive qualities, including being very personable and charming. His teachers loved him, despite that fact that he was not performing very well in their classes. Although he struggled, Rick worked hard, and his teachers, following his lead, also worked hard. They gave him extra help both before and after school, checked his notes when asked, and gave him extra attention, going back over his homework and correcting his mistakes. Although his grades were still not very good, everyone involved felt that Rick was at least learning and making progress and passing all his classes.

Rick's parents, trying to do the right thing and help their son, pushed for him to receive special education. At first the school refused, saying that Rick's grades, though poor, still placed him on grade level. Rick's parents hired a lawyer and put pressure on the school, threatening legal action. After many heated exchanges and a lot of bad blood, the school officials acquiesced, and agreed to provide several very specific services. And they diligently followed through on what they promised. When the semester ended and Rick began the new semester with all new teachers, however, he found that he was treated much differently. Although these new teachers also provided the specific services that were promised him through special education, the extra attention and general support that he had received was no longer there. Rather than focusing on Rick's needs and looking at him as an engaging and enthusiastic student, Rick's new teachers were more concerned with satisfying their obligations and minimum requirements, and viewed him and his parents as difficult. Although both the school and Rick's parents were able to work through this difficult period in the long run, Rick was the one who lost out in the interim.

The point here is not that special education is bad or ineffective, or that special education teachers don't care; in fact we feel just the opposite.

The point is that when teachers, even good teachers, are pushed or forced, they do not teach as well as when they themselves become invested in the student. Thus, rather than trying to force the school into doing what you want, it will probably be more effective to try to develop a good working relationship with the school. Show them that you are not coming in and pointing fingers. Instead, you want to work with the school to solve problems. If you are the parent that the teacher likes hearing from, the conference that they look forward to, then that teacher, and the entire school, will do whatever it takes to teach your son or daughter.

The truth is that most teens are fundamentally good kids. Some of them have some difficulties or frustrations that interfere with their performance in school. (If your son or daughter is not a fundamentally good kid, then there are bigger problems to tackle than simply working with the school.) The goal, then, is to form a relationship with the school in order to show this to the teacher, to help them to see your son or daughter in this positive light, as opposed to seeing him or her as lazy or as a pain in the neck. Again, more often than not, in the long run this strategy will yield far greater returns.

Appendix A

Date:	Class:	Class:
Teacher initials: Yesterday's homework turned in		
Teacher initials: Correct assignment recorded		
Teacher initials: Correct materials recorded		
Parent initials: Shown homework assignment		
Parent initials: Shown completed homework		
Parent initials: Homework placed in bookbag		

Put the Teenager Down and Slowly Back Away

Rebellion and Discipline

In American culture—media, literature, and movies, and history—we tend to romanticize those who assert themselves and their views over an authority that doesn't understand, or doesn't care. Raising teenagers means dealing with their age-appropriate assertiveness and sometimes even rebellion. In more extreme cases, however, this can take the form of oppositional behavior, and unfortunately, even violence. This chapter will discuss rebellion, oppositional behavior, sibling rivalry, and teenage violence, as well as discipline strategies to help parents address and cope with these behaviors.

Rebellion and Oppositional Behavior

As we've discussed, conflict between parents and teenagers is inevitable. It represents the teen's need not only to assert himself and his views, but also to try to take responsibility and control of himself. In a sense, it is a teenager's way of destroying and ripping apart his past infantile relationships to replace these relationships with more mature, healthy, and appropriate ones. For parents, therefore, rather than trying stop or prevent rebellion, it may be more reasonable to help the teenager to rebel or to assert his independence in a more mature, responsible, and constructive manner. In other words, he can disagree with you, but you want him to be responsible and respectful about it. And as we discussed in Chapter 4, you want to confine these conflicts to disagreements, rather than allowing them to escalate into arguments or fights. In this sense, rebellion is not something to be avoided as much as it is a difficult time period during which teenagers need their parents' help to learn how to negotiate and handle conflict responsibly.

In contrast to rebellion, some teenagers go as far as to be oppositional. Whereas rebellion is a teenager's assertion of herself towards a specific direction or goal ("I want to stay out later and I don't care what you say!"), oppositional behavior is directed away from or against something. The teen is not moving *toward* what she wants but rather *against* what her parent wants. If the parent says black, the teenager says white. If the parent roots for the New York Yankees, the teen will become a Boston Red Socks fan. Oppositional behavior differs from rebellion in that it by nature dependent, as opposed to being a drive towards independence. Although it offers an illusion of independence, in reality, oppositionalism is quite reactive, since one cannot oppose anything without an authority to oppose.

As we will discuss later, there is a place for dealing with your son or daughter's actual behaviors and the words and attitudes he or she expresses towards you and your spouse. If you focus solely on these behaviors, however, you will fail to address what is driving these behaviors in the first place. In addition, parents must also focus on this dependence/independence issue. Very similar to parenting toddlers, parents of teenagers are in a position of having to help their adolescents learn how to express their independence in helpful, appropriate ways. Most parents are in the unenviable position of needing to provide structure and security while at the same time helping their teenagers to be more independent and to express this independence.

Parents who allow themselves to be put in the position of trying to win conflicts with their teenagers may be playing right into their teenagers' oppositionalism. In these cases, the parent feels trapped. Either they give in to their teenager and abdicate their role and responsibility (not a good option), or they end up pushing back against the teenager and invite more oppositionalism, (also not a pleasant option). To prevent teens from being oppositional (and therefore dependent), it's often helpful for parents remove themselves from the conflict, rather than allowing themselves to be drawn into these struggles. It's much more difficult for teenagers to push against parents if parents take the stance of trying to resolve issues, rather than trying to win, It's harder for a teenager to push if the parent refuses to play the game.

This idea of setting up appropriate structure, while at the same time fostering independence, speaks to the different styles of communication and parenting discussed in Chapter 4. The Authoritarian style of parenting we discussed describes a parenting style that is highly structured and has very clear, direct expectations for the teenager. This particular parenting style also allows—in fact, enables—the teenager to be quite dependent, rather than fostering autonomy. In this way, it almost predisposes the teenager towards oppositionalism or other types of dependent behavior. Although very appropriate in many instances, this parenting style draws clear battle lines between teenagers and parents and pushes the teenager to be oppositional to try to test these guidelines.

In contrast, the Authoritative parenting style also provides a very clear structure for the teenager. The Authoritative style has much more communication, however, and it also helps to foster independence. This parenting style provides structure for the teenager and sets up a *collaborative* relationship between parent and teen. It does not blur the boundaries between the two, and does not in any way invalidate or undermine the hierarchy in the family. Rather, it sets the parent up as the authority figure, but an authority figure who is on the same side as the teenager, not one that is in opposition to the teenager. Because it is clear who's in charge, this enables parents to be less reactive, For example, when dealing with oppositionalism, you can move beyond the *content* of the disagreement, to focus on the *process* of how your son or daughter disagrees and pushes against you.

Sibling Rivalry

One specific potential cause of rebellion and strife in a family is sibling rivalry. It's very tempting to generalize about what causes strife or tension among siblings, when in actuality the specifics of one situation may have nothing to do with the relationships of a different family. There are, however, some general themes to bear in mind when trying to cope with tension among brothers and sisters.

Certainly a great deal of sibling rivalry and sibling tension is about what is going on between the actual siblings. Research has shown, however, that a lot of what is going on between parents or between parents and siblings may affect the siblings' relationship with each other. For example, research has shown that the more marital stress there is in a family, the more sibling rivalry there is in a family, and vice versa. Similarly, there is a correlation between a sibling's need for attention from the parents and tension between siblings. Please note that correlation does not mean causation; these parental factors are not necessarily causing the tension and difficulties between or among brothers and sisters. Even though these factors may not be causal factors, however, helping to improve the tension between parents, or having parents provide more attention to one or both siblings, can often be very useful in helping to alleviate rivalry and tension among siblings.

Sibling rivalry may also be related to the relative roles that different individuals have within a family. In all families, various family members have various roles. There's the strict parent, the lenient parent, the smart child, the athletic child, the good child, the black sheep. Without realizing it, parents often play into these roles and reinforce these roles in how they talk with their children and how they compare one to the other. Sibling rivalry can often be a reflection of these roles and a process by which to help maintain these roles. If parents can be cognizant and sensitive to their children being pigeonholed in certain roles and do what they can to break them out of these rigid and stifling roles, this may help to relieve tensions between siblings.

Finally, sibling rivalry can be related to how brothers and sisters compare themselves with each other. Among spouses, research has shown that one spouse being successful can either be helpful or harmful to the other spouse. If one spouse is successful in an area that is important to the other spouse's sense of who they are and sense of self-worth, then the second spouse will often feel resentful and competitive, or sometimes even belittled, by the first spouse. For example, if both husband and wife are psychologists, and one is a more successful psychologist, then one might feel resentful and competitive of the other. In contrast, if one spouse is successful in an area that is valued by the second spouse, but not integral to that spouse's sense of self-worth and identity, then this does not foster competition and resentment. In fact, the second spouse may feel bolstered and supported by this other spouse's success, as in this case, one spouse's achievement is a positive reflection on the other spouse. These same patterns may be true with siblings. If two siblings have the same interests—if they both play piano or if they both swim or they're both writers—and one is better than the other, this can foster resentment and competition. If two brothers or sisters have different interests, however, then one sibling's success can actually make the other sibling feel better about herself. Therefore, it's often very helpful and very healthy to encourage siblings not just to follow in their older brothers' or sisters' footsteps, but also to develop their own unique interests and skills.

Aggression, Violence, and Anger Management

Especially given events of recent years, few things worry parents of teenagers as much as the potential for violence. What contributes to teenage violence, and what can parents do to intervene? A number of behaviors in children and younger adolescents may indicate that the child may become violent as an older teenager. Often, these tendencies first come out in terms of verbal abuse and verbal lashing out at home. This is usually followed by similar verbal aggression from the child in a context outside of the home. The child may then progress to vandalism or physical aggression directed at inanimate objects or animals, and finally, to physical violence directed at other individuals.

How and when should parents intervene? Certainly, parents must work to stop aggressive behaviors and promote more positive behaviors. And teens must be held accountable for their behaviors, made to face consequences and make amends. But parents must also recognize that the behaviors that the child or teenager performs are an outward manifestation of emotional factors, and that those emotional factors must be addressed if the child's behavior is going to change permanently.

Verbal abuse, vandalism, and physical violence are the behaviors of individuals who do not know how to express their anger in a constructive manner. As a result, this anger is let out in violent, aggressive, and destructive means. Parents need to help children and teens learn to deal with these negative, angry feelings, and to teach them how to express these feelings in a more controlled, modulated, and healthy manner.

Let's illustrate this with an example. Imagine two balloons blown up to the same size. They have the same amount of air inside of them. Now, take a Swiss Army knife, and with the point of the blade, poke a hole in one of the balloons. It will burst, and the balloon will be destroyed. It makes a big pop, and we have little bits of rubber balloon all over the floor. Now take the second balloon. Take the end where it is tied off, put it in your mouth, and pull the balloon tight. If you take the blade of the Swiss Army knife and make a small incision in the balloon right where it's pulled taut, it won't burst. Rather, all the air will rush out of the balloon. (If you are a teenager, you'll notice that this makes a silly sound.) The second balloon is not destroyed, and in fact, it's possible to blow this balloon up again and to tie off this new incision.

Each balloon started out with the same amount of air, or interior pressure. In the first case, this pressure was released all at once in an explosive, uncontrolled way, and the balloon was destroyed. In the second case, this same amount of pressure was released in a more modulated fashion, and the balloon survived. The balloon was not destroyed. This is a model for dealing with anger in our children and teenagers. We would love to be able give parents advice that would make the anger, frustration, and negative feelings in their children and teenagers magically disappear. But this is not going to happen. Instead, you need to focus on how to help your teenager express these negative feelings. If these feelings build up until the teenager metaphorically explodes, the result may be violence. If it is taken care of slowly, in a controlled (rather than impulsive) fashion, it will come out in ways that might not be pleasant, but which will certainly be much more manageable and less destructive.

The goal for coping with teenage violence, therefore, can really be restated as helping to provide teenagers with better, more efficient anger management techniques and strategies. In many ways, developing the means to cope with and express their feelings and frustrations is a primary task for any teenager, not simply teens with anger management issues. How many teenagers do you know who *never* have anger management issues? Such struggles are developmentally appropriate and are as much a part of adolescence as acne.

Although these strategies may be different from teenager to teenager, most effective strategies bear a number of similarities that are

worth pointing out. First, allow some time for a cool-down period before trying to actually deal with whatever caused the anger in the first
place. This can be helpful for both teenagers and parents. Second, rather
than telling your teenager that he shouldn't be angry or to stop being
angry (essentially telling them to keep this anger inside), help provide
strategies to get this anger out. This can mean different things for different kids. Some strategies include listening to music, writing, draw-
ing, talking, or doing physical activities like shooting baskets, lifting
weights, or even snapping pencils. For most teenagers, some type of
physical activity that allows them to blow off steam is the most helpful
technique.

After both the teenager and parent have had a chance to calm down
and decompress, then it is a good idea to talk. At this point, and only at
this point, the focus should be on the content of whatever the problem
was. The parent and the teen should discuss solutions to the problem,
and if one is warranted, an appropriate consequence or a punishment
for the violent or destructive behavior. It's also important to work with
the teenager to identify what exactly is making them angry or frustrated and how they might be able to handle these types of situations
differently in the future. Also, it might be helpful to discuss other methods for calming down and blowing off steam (again when everyone is
already calm), especially if it's taking quite a bit of work and time to get
to this point. Finally, parents should examine their interactions both
with other adults and with their kids, and focus on what they themselves are modeling to the teenager. It doesn't do much good for a parent to lose his temper and rant and rave and punch the wall and yell at
the top of his lungs for his teenager to calm down. As parents, we need
to take our own advice and to model exactly what we would like our
teenagers to do. You will have more credibility and be more effective if
you hold yourself to the same or even higher standards than those to
which you hold your teen.

In addition to all these emotional factors, when dealing with violence, it is important for parents to focus on maintaining the hierarchy
of the family. Parents cannot feel intimidated, constrained, or held hos-
tage by their teen's anger. Parents must have the freedom and confidence, not to "break" their angry teenagers, but to help them learn to

better cope with their frustrations. Teenagers must view their parents as strong enough to be useful and valuable resources, as opposed to a weaker force that may be easily trampled or sidestepped.

Finally, in dealing with anger and violence, the issue of medication arises. Medication can be very helpful in helping teenagers to deal with serious anger management issues, and it can be a necessary and effective component of treatment. But medications can also mask the anger and the frustration that teenagers feel, thereby preventing them from learning how to express and cope with these negative feelings. Medication is less an alternative to expressing and dealing with these types of emotions than it is an aid in making it easier to cope with them.

Discipline

Given everything we've talked about so far in this chapter, how do parents discipline their teenagers? First, let us be clear: when we discuss discipline, we are not just talking about punishment. All children and teenagers need some form of structure, and punishment may sometimes have to be part of that. If, however, we define discipline as a scenario in which the goal is for teens to behave in the way we would like them to behave (and not behave in way in which we do not want them to behave), discipline is much more than punishment. Effective discipline encompasses communication, reinforcement, and praise. Even when disciplining (especially when disciplining), your goal should be to provide at least two or three times as many positive as negative comments to your teenager. As we've discussed, punishment only tells a teenager what *not* to do. It does not tell a teenager what to do instead. By contrast, reinforcement and praise teach a teenager what you *would* like them to do. Punishment alone is not nearly as effective as punishment combined with positive reinforcement when teenagers meet expectations and perform well.

For example, Scott was a high-school sophomore whose older brother had come home from college. One evening, Scott's brother kept pushing and poking Scott. Scott tried asking him to stop, and he tried to ignore it, but his brother just continued with his playful bullying.

Finally, Scott snapped, and he picked up a glass and threw it at his brother. When Scott's father brought Scott into a family therapy session, he was furious. "Scott should not, under any circumstances, have thrown that glass," he said. "There is no excuse for that!" And Scott's father was right; Scott should not have thrown the glass. After a few minutes, the therapist asked Scott's father what Scott should have done. The father replied that Scott definitely should not have thrown the glass. "Yes," the therapist persisted, "but what should he have done instead?" The father and therapist went back a forth a few times "He should *not* have thrown the glass!" "But what *should* he have done?" Finally, the father said, exasperated, "I don't know what he should have done, but he should not throw a glass at his brother!" And that, very specifically, was the point. Scott didn't know what else he should have done either.

Sometimes this is a difficult question, with no obvious answer for parents or teenagers. Scott was punished, and rightfully so. But the disciplining should not have stopped there. Scott's father also needed to help Scott figure out what to do instead. Scott and his father decided that the appropriate response would have been to physically walk away when his brother started with him. To make this stick in the future, Scott's father decided that he needed to notice and praise Scott for doing the right thing and walking away. In fact, Scott's father needed to go out of his way to praise Scott for coexisting with his brother for a period of time without getting into a fight. To take this even further, despite the fact that Scott threw the glass at his brother, Scott should be praised for first trying to handle it in a better way and asking his brother several times to stop.

This may seem awkward, even condescending, for parents. You may be thinking, "You mean I have to say 'thanks for not getting into a fight with your brother' or 'thanks for trying not to get into a fight with your brother'—shouldn't that be obvious?" Remember, the question of what Scott should have done instead did not have an obvious answer. If Scott's parents wanted him to learn to handle these situations differently, then they needed to reinforce and praise him whenever he did so. If your teen does not want you to say anything, if she does feel that this is condescending, then praising her in this way is not reinforcing or rewarding and she will tell you that. Even in this case, however, at the very least you will be showing your teen that you are trying to notice the positive things she is doing as well as the negatives.

The first goal in disciplining a teenager is to be proactive rather than reactive. If your discipline and your consequences are simply a response to what the teenager does, then the teenager is essentially in charge and the entire hierarchy of the family is turned upside-down. You can only deal with the content of the situation—in this case, providing discipline, structure, and sometimes even punishment—when you and your teen have calmed down.

One of the things we hear frequently is that parents must punish their children immediately after they misbehave or transgress. Although this may be a good general strategy, it's less important for teenagers than it is for young children. Because of their verbal skills and their general cognitive development, teenagers can still pair a punishment with their misbehavior even if one does not follow immediately after the other. This is important to remember because it provides parents of teenagers with the luxury of time, not just to calm themselves down, but to discuss what's going to happen to ensure that they're in agreement. One father came into our office and said that his daughter had missed curfew, and in a fit of rage, he had grounded the teenager for six months. In our office, the father said, "I made a mistake. I didn't mean to do that. I don't want to ground her for six months, but what do I do? I can't back down now." Rather than finding yourself in this type of situation, it is often much better to take some time before disciplining your teenager, and to discuss the discipline with the other parent. Remember, the other parent is in the position of having to support your decision and your punishment, and this will be much easier if you both agree on the punishment beforehand, rather than asking the other parent to enforce a punishment with which they disagree.

Think of the purposes of consequences. Sometimes a consequence is meant to punish, but there are other reasons for providing consequences as well, including showing your teenager that you're taking something seriously, and to highlight and support the hierarchy in the family. In most cases, shorter punishments serve these purposes just as well as longer punishments. They may not be as punitive, but often they are just as effective. They are also much easier for the parent to follow through on and administer. Teenagers often look at the severity of a punishment in comparison to past punishments. When devising an appropriate punishment, always remember to leave yourself some room to escalate if the punishment does not seem to be working.

For example, when Karen's parents received an e-mail from one of Karen's teachers that she had not turned in a homework assignment, they grounded her until the end of the marking period. This backfired in two ways. First, it made Karen feel that she had nothing left to lose and provided no incentive for her to do her homework for the rest of the marking period. *Why bother?*, she thought. *It won't help anyway.* Second, when Karen again failed to turn in her homework, her parents had very few options left to punish this second transgression. If grounding her for one marking period didn't work, then there was little reason to believe that grounding her for two marking periods would be any more effective. Karen's parents now found themselves in the position of feeling that they had take something else away, even though they really didn't want to. A more effective strategy might have been to ground Karen for only one week to begin with, leaving room to ground her for another week (or maybe even two weeks) the next time. Never back yourself into a corner where you feel that you don't have any other options. If this does happen, you'll find yourself in a reactive position, as opposed to feeling in control and proactive.

Remember, the goal of discipline is not simply to control behavior, but also to teach and reinforce communication, and to teach teenagers how to deal with problems and conflict as they come up. How the teenager handles his or her transgression is maybe more important than what the actual transgression was in the first place. Good discipline helps teenagers discuss the problem, take responsibility for it, and make amends appropriately, as opposed to simply being punished for the behavior, which only makes them feel helpless and defensive. Thus, the process of discipline (being honest, taking responsibility, and owning your own mistakes) is just as important as the content of punishment.

CHAPTER 8

DRUGS, SEX, AND ROCK 'N ROLL

Discussing the Tough Stuff, Including (Gasp!) Your Own Adolescence

During a recent high school PTA program where one of us was speaking, a student commented while looking around the auditorium that the attendance was sparse. He said that in elementary and middle school, attendance at PTA meetings was nearly 100%. He commented that it was ironic that at such a dangerous period in their children's lives, parents would cease to participate in programs designed to help them support their teenagers and keep them safe.

I later thought about that astute observation and tried to consider the cause, for it was accurate for almost all high schools. Were parents afraid to confront the current realities in their teenager's lives? Were they resistant to change parenting strategies or reflect on their behaviors and lifestyle? Had they prematurely separated from their youngsters because they didn't know how to parent them and remain connected? This chapter was written to help parents deal with some of the most difficult issues of adolescence.

Drinking and Drug Abuse

Adolescents are ideal targets for alcohol and drug abuse. They are breaking away from parental control, are highly susceptible to peer pressure, see themselves as invulnerable, and are drawn to fun and excitement. This genuinely high-risk period of development is exacerbated if the use and abuse of chemicals is a factor for an adolescent.

Our society is filled with messages that glorify alcohol and drug use. These messages originate from three main sources: parents and their adult friends, the media, and peers. Any one of these sources can stimulate experimentation or regular use. If parents drink regularly or overuse prescription medications, this sends powerful messages to their children. Advertisements and movies are filled with exciting, sexual, and humorous scripts that are associated with alcohol use; beer companies consistently sponsor the most popular Super Bowl commercials; and adults often tell anecdotes detailing someone's foibles while under the influence. Futhermore, a teen's friends may be involved in alcohol or drug use. No matter the source, the attitude conveyed to teens through all of these is that drinking is a cool social activity and that it is easier to have fun when you drink.

Know Your Values

Drug and alcohol use are viewed by many teens as a rite of passage into adulthood. Youngsters are introduced to the substances not by strangers in long dark coats, but by friends, older siblings, cousins, aunts, uncles, and yes, parents and grandparents. Many families have glorified substance use or incorporated it into their celebration, recreation, or relaxation rituals. Many adults regularly use chemicals of some form or another as stress-reduction tools. This combination of parental/adult messages, media bombardment, and peer pressure produces a powerful trifecta that can steer teens into drug and alcohol use. This force, a part of the American landscape for decades now, shows few signs of abating. But acknowledging the prevalence of the problem does not help parents necessarily deal with their own teenagers. Parents are on the front lines of this conflict, and it is vital that they make responsible decisions and communicate these decisions clearly to protect their children from the potential ravages of substance abuse and addiction.

Why shouldn't your teenagers drink when, for years, they have seen adults, including their parents, relax and loosen up by having a few beers? Some teens may perceive the implied double standard as nothing less than a challenge. When we conduct initial assessments, we ask parents, privately, to describe their own personal histories of drug and alcohol use. We observe a common pattern with parents that have used alcohol and other drugs: often, they have not arrived at a clear resolution about their own drug or alcohol use, and therefore, they have given their children mixed messages. Many parents make statements like, "I used, how can I condemn my children for using?," or "My parents couldn't stop me from using, how can anyone stop my kids?," or even, "I turned out okay; I'm sure my teenager will turn out just fine, too." No matter what your own history is, if you as a parent want to protect your teens from accidents, arrest, addiction, and a myriad of problems that substances promote, you must take a firm and consistent stand against substance abuse. Our clinical experiences with substance abuse have brought us in the midst of tragic deaths, severe accidents, family disintegration, lifelong addiction, educational and occupational collapse, serial relationship impairment, and so on—all related to drug abuse. Local judges routinely report that over 80% of all criminal court cases they try are drug or alcohol related in some way.

Talk to your kids early in their lives and often about the harmful effects of substances. Monitor your personal use and be aware of the strong messages from the greater culture that glorify drug and alcohol use.

Melissa, 17 years old, lost her mom to cancer two months before she entered therapy. She was a senior in high school and planning to graduate with a B average and enroll in college for the fall. She was living with her mom's sister and her husband when she started therapy. Melissa reported having a steady boyfriend of 10 months with whom she spent most of her free time.

When Melissa started therapy she had difficulty identifying goals she was interested in achieving. Her aunt stated that she had a great deal of conflict with her husband, Melissa's uncle, and that she was emotionally distant from them. We started Melissa in group and individual therapy, which she accepted readily.

These sessions quickly helped Melissa to open up. She reported that she smoked marijuana with her boyfriend and that they were sexually active. She also reported that her aunt was aware of both behaviors but Melissa had sworn to her not to tell her uncle. Melissa reported further that her uncle was ill-tempered and unemployed. He was also very argumentative, so she spent as much time away from home as possible.

When the adolescent group confronted her on her drug use and voiced their concern, Melissa rationalized the behavior by explaining that her uncle smoked pot regularly and her aunt did occasionally. After steady urging by the group to try and stop, Melissa set a goal to not smoke for one week. This goal was extended each week until she had stopped for five weeks. She reported feeling less depressed, more motivated and energetic, and more aware of her emotions. She had even approached her aunt about her drug use and her husband's drug use in their home.

Melissa stopped coming to therapy two weeks later and didn't return phone calls for a month. Eventually, we were able to make contact. Melissa said she wasn't getting a lot out of therapy and that she and her aunt had decided that her problems had improved and she would not be returning. We asked Melissa if she had resumed smoking pot, which she affirmed. She really did not think that smoking posed a problem for her any longer, however. We suggested we make a last appointment to terminate the treatment, but she declined.

Melissa was influenced to abuse drugs by poor adult modeling and peer pressure. She had not properly grieved for the death of her mother (and early childhood abandonment by her father.) She was self-medicating by smoking frequently and not maturing emotionally. When confronted with her own involvement in Melissa's drug use and resultant problems, her aunt stopped supporting therapy, and Melissa soon returned to her earlier habits.

In our culture, no period of emotional growth is more dynamic than adolescence. Teens experience emotions and sensations in greater breadth and intensity than at any other time in their lives. In addition, most teenagers, whether they admit it or not, are somewhat nervous or apprehensive about what their futures will be like and what their adult lives will bring. If, during this period of development, teens use substances that either blunt or exaggerate the intensity of their sensations—or separate them from adults or peers who can help them identify and articulate these emotions—adolescents will have a significantly more difficult time pursuing their goals and becoming independent. Drug and alcohol use restricts teens' emotional maturation and development, and therefore inhibits their ability to make responsible decisions.

In addition to the threat of physical and/or psychological addiction, to which a certain percentage of individuals who use substances will succumb, substance abuse can become a self-medication process in which the individual attempts to balance a biochemical or neurochemical abnormality, such as generalized anxiety, depression, or bipolar disorder. Drug use can mask these disorders and prevent appropriate mental health treatment for these individuals. Furthermore, the side effects of street drugs can compound the emotional instability and multiply teens' behavioral and mental health problems.

What to do if a Problem Develops

If you suspect that your teen has developed a drug or alcohol problem, don't ignore the situation—it usually gets worse. We advise parents to investigate further. Check your adolescent's room for drugs, alcohol, or paraphernalia. Reflect on recent behavior, mood, and relationship changes. Have your son or daughter's grades dropped, friends changed, activities altered? Check with other parents; they may have heard something from their son or daughter about your child. School counselors, teachers, or administrators spend all day with your teen and are often good sources of information. They also know the peer patterns at school and may know whether a student that experiments with drugs if your teen's peer group is known to experiment with drugs or alcohol.

A typical warning sign for teenage drinking or substance abuse is a decrease in the amount of openness and an increase in the amount of distance between you and your child. Her grades may drop and she may change her friends or activities. When you initiate conversations or questions about her activities or friends she may become angry, defensive, or avoidant. You may notice your teen lying about events or her whereabouts.

It is always wise to know what your teen is doing, where she is and with whom she is spending time. What is she doing after school (a common time to become involved with alcohol or drugs)? Parents should supervise high-school parties, and you should establish a family rule you will be calling a parent in any household where your teen plans to spend the night or attend a party before she has permission to go. During this conversation, include questions about that parent's rules regarding underage drinking.

We recommend parents establish a set of family rules upon which both parents agree and which communicate to their child starting in middle school. Let teens know (with both parents present and later separately) that this issue is very important and substance abuse problems can lead to serious consequences for them or their friends. Let your adolescent know that you will maintain supervision and structure in his life throughout middle and high school to keep him safe and to maintain a close family relationship. This structure should be secure and consistent enough to provide parents information about their youngster's activities and whereabouts.

If a problem concerning lying or substance use occurs, talk to your teen and consider tightening the structure and accountability for a while until trust and communication are restored. If you need help reestablishing communication, consider family counseling. Keep communicating the importance of the issue and your firm commitment to keep them safe.

Sometimes teens become entrenched in drug or alcohol use before parents are aware of it. In this case, increased structure and attempts at building back trust and communication may fail. In such cases, outpatient or inpatient drug therapy, along with regular drug testing, may be the most sensible next step. In a few cases, these measures don't successfully address the substance abuse problems, and residential treatment may be necessary.

Above all, don't separate yourself from your child too early because you feel helpless and don't know what to do. These are serious issues, especially after your teen or his friends have their drivers' licenses. Don't avoid seeking help or just being appropriately involved in your child's high school if things get sticky and relationships conflicts get out of hand. It's far easier for professionals to help families and adolescents early in these problems than after they have become entrenched.

Teenagers generally believe that drinking or getting high is no big deal, and they do not realize the danger they are in or just how far they have fallen until they get in trouble with the law, develop an addiction, or a caring individual—or even a tragic even—opens their eyes. Therefore, parents must remain watchful and involved. Above all, do *not* ignore the warning signs. Inaction and denial enable your youngster and can lead to tragic consequences for them and agony for you.

Sexuality

For adolescents and young adults, sexual behavior can be the most life-changing emotional, social, or physical experience they encounter. Two-thirds of our teens are sexually active by the end of high school. One quarter of sexually active teens will contract a STD (Alan Guttmacher Institute, 1999). The subject of sexuality and the consequences for our adolescents should not be ignored.

Many of our adolescent patients who come in for therapy who are pregnant, or who are adolescent fathers-to-be find themselves burdened with decisions and stresses that they are not equipped to handle. It's also common for adolescents and young adults come into our offices with sexually transmitted diseases (STDs). Sometimes these diseases are not curable, which causes terrible anxiety, shame, and pressure for the teen. Often, the sexual encounter occurred when one or both of the individuals were under the influence of alcohol or drugs. Sometimes, also, pregnancy and/or STDs are the result of date rape, which has extremely traumatic emotional and physical ramifications.

Even under relatively positive and healthy circumstances, sexual activity is not simply a physical or hormonal issue, but one that creates powerful social and emotional complications for teens. Early sexual experiences lead to greater social stress among peers. Although sexually promiscuous teenage boys are today commonly referred to as "hos," "players," "dirty," and so on, the double standard remains alive and well. Generally, girls and young women are much more stigmatized than their male counterparts when their peers find out that they are sexually active. In contrast, males continue to be admired by their peers and to grow in social stature as a result of their sexual exploits. This complicates peer relationships and can hijack teens' attention, time, self-esteem, and confidence.

The best treatment for these difficult problems is prevention, and the best method of prevention is *early and ongoing* discussion, communication, and information about sexuality. You would never fathom letting your 16-year-old drive an automobile without proper education, practice, and supervision. Yet many parents routinely allow their teenage children to date, even go off to college, with little information about the facts and complexities of sexual behavior.

Dan was a senior in high school attending our adolescent group. He entered the group one evening very agitated and stressed. When asked why he was upset, he stated that his girlfriend was pregnant and he did not know what they were going to do. As the group started buzzing with their opinions and questions, we asked if she had obtained a reliable pregnancy test. Dan said he was pretty sure that she was pregnant. We asked him when the last time they had sex was, and he stated that they had not had sex. The group became quiet and we asked Dan why he thought she would be pregnant. Dan stated that they had gotten into a huge fight and his girlfriend was very upset. She was already 10 days late for her period and he knew that if she missed her period because she was emotionally distraught that she would be pregnant. We asked him how he had learned that information, and he stated "health class."

Clearly, Dan and his girlfriend had not acquired very much information about reproduction or sexuality. We frequently find that teenagers know surprisingly little about sexuality and may have significant misinformation about it. We also often find that the percentage of teens who have not talked to their parents about sex and sexuality is greater than those who have.

When we ask parents, "When you were growing up, what was communicated to you about sex and your parents' expectation of your sexual behavior?" most look blank. Some can't even fathom the question; others can't bring themselves to openly talk about the topic. The overwhelming response is "nothing" or "very little." Sometimes their parents referred them to a book; more often, they got their information elsewhere—a high school health class or their peers. The reality is that most parents in past generations did not talk to their children or adolescents about sexuality or what they considered to be appropriate sexual behavior. This pattern of underinforming children about sexuality continues in present-day parenting.

Even if parents do attempt to talk to their teens about sexuality, the conversation often becomes strained and difficult because the subject stirs up shame, embarrassment, and anxiety between parent and child, and the discussions quickly deteriorate into laughter or other avoidance mechanisms. Many parents simply avoid the topic or drop it after a single attempt. But your child's anxiety will be reduced if you become comfortable talking about this topic. Regular discussions on the topic of sexuality can and should occur from early childhood throughout young adulthood. Age-appropriate communication can start with toddlers about not approaching strangers or what to do if strangers approach them. Most parents know how to talk to their toddler about private parts (parts of their bodies covered by a bathing suit) and explain to them that besides the child herself, only parents or doctors, are allowed to touch her in those areas. Once their child is a preteen or a teenager, however, this becomes much more difficult for many parents.

We suggest that parents seek books and films and review school health class materials to begin open and informative discussions with their children at each appropriate age. Elementary-age children are generally receptive to instructive information about appropriate and inappropriate touching. This is also a good age to begin general discussions about age-appropriate sexual contact. During late elementary school and early middle school, many youngsters pick up significant information or misinformation about sexuality from peers, movies, television, family conversations, and so on. It's important that parents communicate healthy values about sexuality before youngsters form their own conceptions from media or their peer group. The subject of sexuality can be much more comfortable to communicate if it becomes a regular exchange between parents and their youngsters. We have frequently been pleasantly surprised by the ease with which adolescents discuss the subject in their peer therapy groups, and the fact that these issues are often easily transferable into family therapy sessions. They are willing and ready to discuss these topics at home, if only their parents take advantage of this opportunity and talk with them. It is truly an understatement to say that an ounce of prevention is worth a pound of cure!

One factor that adults often overlook in discussing teenage sexual behavior is the emotional component. Many teens who are sexually active report that they are genuinely in love with their partner, or at least have strong feelings for him or her. Whether or not what they are experiencing is truly love is irrelevant. The fact is that they feel that their emotions are genuine, and they deserve to have their feelings taken seriously and not discounted or belittled. This is not to say that being in love as a teenager gives one a license to become sexually active, but these emotional factors can be a very important part of their motivation. As such, you must address your teen's emotions, not just her behavior. It is normal and natural, even healthy, for most teenagers to experience, their emotions very intensely. Help them to learn how to express, experience, and share these feelings with others in other, healthy and adaptive ways.

As children reach their adolescent years, it's important that they hear from their parents how their bodies are changing inside and outside. We have many female clients that were "surprised" by their first menstrual cycle. Talk to your preteen and teen about their changes, including hormonal activity. Explain to them how hormones generate sexual and affectionate desire and that they might feel great pleasure with physical contact. It's important to help them establish and be able to articulate limits on this desire and behavior while helping them understand the social, relationship, and health consequences of such contact.

Alexis, age 12, was brought into our office by her parents. She had been caught writing a note to her boyfriend while she was in Science class. Her teacher glanced at the note and read that Alexis had been meeting her boyfriend in the school bathroom and having intercourse. The teacher gave the note to the school guidance counselor, who then shared it with the principal. A parent conference at school resulted in Alexis having completely restricted contact with her boyfriend and teacher-supervised visits to the bathroom. Within a week, nearly every student at her school had become aware of the sexual encounters and restriction. Alexis was shunned by her peers (many who had previously known and had already distanced themselves from her) and treated suspiciously by school staff. We recommended to the family that they begin family counseling immediately and have Alexis start individualized counseling with a female therapist. The family therapist opened communication with the school staff to coordinate Alexis's treatment. We recommended an adolescent pediatrician from whom Alexis could obtain a physical and good medical information.

Alexis was put on phone restriction at home and told not to contact her boyfriend for two months. During this period of restriction, Alexis participated in numerous therapy, medical, school, and family sessions helping her understand the social, family, physical, and emotional consequences of her sexual behavior and decisions. It became increasingly clear that her parents had never had any discussions with Alexis about sexuality and sexual activity and in fact that her parents had never talked about nor even agreed on the family values concerning sexuality. Her older sister, a junior in high school, participated in family sessions and stated that she had also had few, if any discussions with her parents on these topics. Alexis participated very bravely in all the meetings, and although she was very angry and sometimes defiant, she was eventually able to reconnect with her family and many peers at school.

Initially, it might be difficult to start these conversations, but both parents need to help their teens understand the connection between emotional, social, and physical pressures involved with sexual activity with another person. Early sexual contact between teenagers can have immediate and lifelong consequences that children are not at all prepared to handle, and these consequences may alter their future dramatically.

Your discussions should be detailed. You should discuss pregnancy, and you may wish to discuss contraception. You should also discuss STDs and how is each transmitted. You should certainly discuss what constitutes sexual activity as far as you are concerned—intercourse, oral sex, petting, kissing? You should discuss the age at which and circumstances under which you would consider it appropriate for your adolescent to engage in these different levels of sexual activity. If you believe that he should delay sex until he is truly in love, or supporting himself on his own, married, or has achieved another milestone, express this. Your teen may not comply with your wishes entirely, but they will likely have some effect.

Always try to make the conversation natural, relaxed, and age-appropriate. Relying exclusively upon others—teachers, religious teachings, health care providers, or peers—is inviting misinformation and crisis. As parents, we must take responsibility for our children's health, education, and values.

It's Not Like You Didn't Do It!

Talking with Your Teenager About Your Involvement with Drugs, Alcohol, and Sex in High School

Some questions strike fear into the hearts of all parents. When our children are young, it might be "Why does it rain?" or "Why is the sky blue?." As they grow older, it might be questions about why a particular event occurred, or how to do long division. But it has been our experience that one group of questions raises more anxiety and uncertainty in parents than any other query: "Did you smoke pot (or do drugs, drink, have sex) when you were in high school?" It's not that we, as parents, don't know the answers. We do. In fact, lately, it is one of the few questions that we are able to answer, even if we can't bring ourselves to answer out loud. Then why is it so difficult to tell our teenagers the truth?

These are not simple issues, and highlight many of the most vexing and frustrating challenges of raising teenagers in today's anything-but-simple world. But answering these questions also provides one of the best opportunities to improve your relationship and communication with your teenager.

If you honestly did not drink or experiment with drugs or have sex as a teenager, there generally is no difficulty discussing these facts with your children. The problem arises if, like many people, you did in fact drink, smoke, or do other things that you do not wish your children to emulate. If you did, you may feel that your past actions are inconsistent with your current beliefs, that you now look at things differently from when you were a teenager; that you have changed our views and your priorities, and that, in short, you made a mistake. Frequently, the parents we see in our practice tell us that they are as worried about mistakes that they made in the past as they are about giving their children the "best answer" to cope with issues and questions today. They feel ashamed or guilty; they worry that they are a disappointment or even a failure. They fear that they will lose their family's respect if they were to find out. If you have made similar mistakes, rather than being reasons to avoid discussion, these are precisely the reasons to talk about your past and how you have accepted and coped with your actions. Remember, no one can be a perfect parent; rather, we can only become more comfortable being imperfect and making mistakes. You need only to strive to try to be a better parent, to learn from your mistakes, and to be, as D.W. Winnicott has termed, a "good enough" parent.

WHY TELL YOUR TEEN ABOUT YOUR MISTAKES?

The anxiety-provoking topic of your conduct when you were a teenager is actually a very useful and powerful tool for teaching your child. Remember, your teen will learn how to cope with this and similar situations both by watching how you cope with your uneasiness, and by how you help him or her cope with their uneasiness.

In effect, by talking about the mistakes you made in your youth, you are putting your money where your mouth is. How would you like your children to handle their experimentations or temptations in this area? How would you like them to address and handle any one of the several thousand mistakes they will likely make during the rest of their lives? Although there will be differences from parent to parent and from family to family, we find that most parents' answers to these questions contain some central themes:

1. We would like our children to recognize and identify their mistakes, not to deny or avoid them.

2. We would like them to accept responsibility for their mistakes. Responsibility, after all, is one of the chief themes, goals and concerns of parents who bring their adolescents to our practice. How many times have we told children that if they had told the truth in the beginning, they would not have gotten in trouble, that lying about a transgression is often worse than the transgression itself?

3. We would also like them to learn from their mistakes and to atone for them.

4. We would like our teens to see that it is all right to discuss one's mistakes or difficulties with others, and when necessary, to ask for help.

5. Finally, we would like them to see that, when all is said and done, a mistake is simply that, a mistake. If handled correctly, maturely, responsibly, a mistake is something that they can put behind them. It does not have to affect the rest of their lives, future decisions, how other people look at them, or how they may come to look at themselves.

Rather than helping your teen avoid a difficult topic, your role is to try to create and demonstrate an emotionally safe environment that will allow them to discuss these same confusing and frustrating issues. If you would like your children to be able to come clean and take responsibility for what they have done, you must be able to pave the way yourself.

This strategy is often much, much more difficult to actually put into practice than it is to dream up in the first place. Despite the rationale, it often makes us feel uncomfortable to actually discuss our own mistakes and shortcomings. If this is difficult for adults, with all our maturity and resources, however, consider how difficult it is for a teenager to discuss their mistakes and temptations.

The Actual Discussion

You probably would not have made it this far as a parent if you did not already have a good understanding of your son or daughter. Therefore, follow your own instincts when having "the discussion" with your teenager. These are guidelines and suggestions, but can be modified to apply to your particular family and your personal style.

Remember, however, that when you discuss anything with your teenagers, that they have an agenda as well, and their agenda does not necessarily agree with yours. One reason to discuss this and other topics with your teens is to improve your relationship and your communication with them. One of the adolescent's completely natural and healthy goals is to assert his or her independence and to separate from us, however. Thus, even the most well-prepared discussions sometimes turn out to be significantly more difficult than we had anticipated.

First, you must model for your teens how to address and discuss their involvement, or potential involvement, with drugs and alcohol. Demonstrate for them exactly how to do what you will soon be asking of them. During this discussion, they will pick up on how you are feeling; teenagers have a certain radar when it comes to what adults, and especially parents, tell them. They know when we are being truthful, when we are talking down to them, when we are being sarcastic, when we are afraid of them, and when we are trying to manipulate them. It's better that your son or daughter see that what you are doing may be difficult, perhaps embarrassing, but that it's at least genuine. He or she will also see that you are discussing this topic despite your uneasiness, that you are not using your own fears and insecurities as an excuse to avoid a difficult issue. You will show them how to take responsibility and help them to do the same.

As is the case with most parental interventions, it is preferable to discuss your history with drugs and alcohol on your terms. That is, when you are asked about what you did when you were in high school, do not feel pressured to answer right away before you have had a chance to collect your thoughts. When you are ready, then and only then should you reopen the subject and discuss the matter. This will allow you to stay calm and to be proactive rather than reactive. This applies not only to parents but to therapists as well. In our practice, we frequently choose to wait until the following session to respond to a question or issue posed by a client, allowing us time to think. When you do respond, give yourself adequate time. If your teen truly wants to hear the answer to his question, he must agree to listen to the entire answer, not just part of it. It is important that your teen understand your full answer and the reasoning behind it, and not misperceive your viewpoint because he heard only part of what you have to say.

In addition, remember to focus on *how* you conduct this discussion. Stay calm, open and genuine. How you address this issue is as important as what you actually say. As we mentioned in Chapter 4, an important part of this process is your nonverbal communication with your teen. It is not enough to simply listen to your adolescent (or to anybody for that matter); you must show him that you are listening. Facial expressions— a nod or smile at the right time—and body language, such as leaning forward in your chair, can show that you are listening, that you are interested, and that you care. This type of communication can often make a more powerful impact, and make it easier to discuss a difficult topic, than anything you actually say.

Tell your teenager about the mistakes that you have made in the past. Often, it is helpful to discuss other faux pas and goofs first, before bringing up drugs and alcohol. Talk about mistakes that, even though they were mistakes, really weren't that bad. In fact, they may even have been fun, though ill advised or just plain stupid. These instances may include the time you thought it would be fun to try and jump your bicycle across a creek, or when you played a practical joke on your sister and got caught. These are mistakes that still make you smile when you think about them, mistakes that you might even make again, given the chance. Then, draw the distinction between these "fun" types of mistakes and other, more serious mistakes. Unfortunately, you have committed these types of mistakes as well. You are not proud of this fact, but it's the truth. These are not funny stories that make you smile when you remember them. You are embarrassed by them. You are not immune to making even serious mistakes, especially when you were younger, but hopefully, you were able to learn from them. Your experimentation with or habitual use of alcohol, pot, or other drugs falls into this category of mistakes. Now that you have set the tone, you are ready to tell your teen some of the things you did when you were a teenager.

After you describe what you did, go on to explain why you look at things differently now. This is nothing to be ashamed of. Describe how your views have changed, and why. Did something happen to make you look at drugs and alcohol differently? What made you change your mind?

Finally, many parents find it helpful to sum up this phase of the conversation by explaining why they have disclosed so much of themselves. This summary not only serves to help keep you, the parent, focused, but also to highlight the important lessons, for your teenager. The second purpose of this summary phase is that it helps to transition the focus away from you and your exploits and back to you son or daughter and what they are currently struggling with in their life. If done skillfully, this discussion may serve as an introduction to a larger discussion on *their* thoughts, practices and temptations concerning drugs, smoking, alcohol, or sex.

The first step in being able to address any difficult or frightening problem is the ability to discuss it. Therefore, this discussion should not begin and end with you and your exploits. It is important for you to take the first step to help guide your teen to follow your example. You want your teen to be honest and open despite his or her discomfort. You know how difficult it is to talk about this topic; after all, you just did so yourself. Your willingness to listen is the critical factor in creating the emotional comfort that allows teens to talk about these difficult topics.

For example, Jack was a 17-year-old patient who was in therapy at our office for a chronic substance abuse problem. He had routinely been smoking marijuana, several times each week, for almost two years. Not surprisingly, Jack's relationship with his parents had suffered considerably, and was almost nonexistent. They fought constantly, and both Jack and his parents admitted that neither side listened to the other anymore. After accomplishing nothing for several therapy sessions, we suggested to Jack's mother that she talk with Jack about her drug use during high school. Her first reaction was to become angry and defensive. Why should she air her dirty laundry? After all, she said, this wasn't about her, but about Jack. With some coaxing and coaching, she finally agreed. Jack's mother began a session by telling her son that it wasn't fair to always focus on him and his mistakes, and that maybe she should have to explain to him some of her mistakes. She talked about different mistakes she had made in the past, both not-so-serious and serious mistakes. She then told him about the drugs she had done when she was his age, and that this was, in her opinion, a *bad* mistake. While she was speaking, Jack truly listened. He watched her, he was quiet, and he asked questions when she paused. This, in and of itself, was a major accomplishment, considering the several previous therapy sessions.

When Jack's mother had finished talking about what she had done, Jack said that he never thought she had understood him before, and that he was surprised by her confession. They talked for the rest of the session, both about what Jack has been doing, and what his mother had done twenty years ago. Nothing was resolved then and there, but they were communicating, talking and listening without fighting, about Jack's drug addiction. To her surprise, Jack's mother found that she was able to discuss this without condoning it, and without lecturing to her son. As the session began to wind down, and the therapist tried to end the session, Jack made a point of interrupting him and said that he needed to ask a question. He then asked his mother how she quit, and they talked about her answer over the next several weeks. Jack, of course, did not quit right then and there, but it was a start.

APPLYING THE LESSON

This general strategy for framing and interpreting our interactions with teenagers can be a very useful and effective tool for addressing various other issues and problems. All parents experience times when their son or daughter has done something or said something, and the parent is not quite sure how to cope with the situation. Very often, this occurs during an argument or a fight. You feel drawn in by your teenager. They have successfully pushed your buttons and you find yourself simply reacting to them on their level, emotionally and impulsively, without a clear idea or plan to proactively address the situation as an adult. (By the way, none of us is immune to this; we all fall into this trap. As trained psychologists who deal with children and teenagers professionally, we sometimes find ourselves being drawn into arguments and fights, and saying really intelligent and helpful things, like "Did not!")

Often, this confusion results, in part, from the teenager imposing some of their rage, frustration and confusion onto the parent. In these situations, it is sometimes easier to be able to see what we think they should do, rather than what we should do. Say you would like your teenager to calm down and listen, and, if she disagrees, to do so respectfully, or whatever the appropriate responses are for that particular situation. Now, apply these suggestions to yourself. Remember, we must deal with our feelings in the same manner that we would like them to deal with theirs, and model for them exactly how to do this.

We often say what we would like our teenagers to do, without fully understanding the difficulty of what we are asking. "Admit it when you make a mistake, even a big mistake." "Don't listen to your friends." "Don't try drugs." Although this is all good advice, it may sometimes be harder to follow than we realize. Following this advice ourselves, in front of our children, helps give us a better understanding of what we are asking them to do, an appreciation of their struggles, some of the pitfalls they may face, and how to help them see to it through.

CHAPTER 9

WHAT KIND OF FAMILY IS THIS, ANYWAY?

Separation, Divorce, and Blended Families

Significant cultural changes transformed American families in the 1960s, '70s, '80s and '90s. One of the consequences of these changes is that approximately one out of every two marriages in the U.S. now ends in divorce (Kreider & Fields, 2002). Some parents marry several times, some live with a partner without marrying, or some may raise a child or children as a single parent.

The effect on children, families, and parenting has been profound. A generation ago, one whispered that a child came from a "broken home" if a divorce occurred, as if this was something so horrific that it could not be said aloud, as if it were something from which a child could not possibly recover. The very term "broken home" implies that the family has been destroyed and that the house, the home, and the security it represents has also been destroyed and split apart. A stigma was attached to children, and one or more parent was faulted for not keeping the family together.

Although divorce itself is a traumatic event for all members of the family, children need not be permanently scarred by the experience if the adults in their lives can handle the situation with maturity and the children's best interests in mind. Today, children and adults accept divorce as more commonplace with less stigma attached. As the numbers of divorced families have increased, so too has the volume of research concerning divorced parents and children of divorced parents.

Two such researchers, Judith Wallerstein and Mavis Hetherington, have followed divorced families decades after their split to determine and examine the effects and consequences years later on the individual family member (Hetherington & Kelly, 2003; Wallerstein, Lewis,& Blakeslee, 2001).

What to Expect Initially

Divorced families with adolescent children face unique problems. Teenagers, of course, are attempting to try out their independence and are beginning to separate from their families. Faced with the challenge of adjusting to the transition of their parents' separation and divorce, adolescents can become overwhelmed and stressed. Most parents should consider getting professional help, given the extreme stressors in families who are undergoing divorce or its aftermath.

Ideally, both parents should maintain a consistent presence, remain vigilant with their teens, communicate as much as possible, provide emotional support, be good role models, and be able to financially support the family. Do your best. This is *not* an easy or ideal world! And remember, parents have needs also. Consider how you are going to remain happy, connected, financially sound and emotionally stable. We'll try and offer some guidelines to help with this unique set of challenges.

Mistakes are inevitable, but they can be instructive. Remember, this is new territory. Anybody would face stressors such as these with decreased capacity and numerous distractions. The first year or two will be particularly difficult, and going through this transition with teenagers will hopefully be only a stage of your child's development, not a permanent condition.

The prospect of divorce is usually a shock to children. Research indicates that a full two-thirds of adolescents had little awareness of their parent's unhappiness prior to the impending separation (Wallerstein, 1979). Adolescents typically do not know why their parents divorced. Parents can be overwhelmed, distressed, and distracted during this period and understandably have difficulty telling their children why they are getting divorced or what the arrangements for the children will be after the separation takes place. Parents often don't know how much detail to give their children about the reasons for the split. Most parents are apprehensive that their children may be unhappy, frightened, angered, or deeply depressed about the separation or divorce and are reluctant to face these negative feelings. As a result, it is also rare that children or adolescents have opportunity to express their concerns or feelings about the impending breakup. In Judith Wallerstein's extensive study of sixty families, not one single family was able to provide the children/adolescent with an adequate opportunity to express their concerns or expectations post divorce (Wallerstein & Kelly, 2001).

Divorce is a loss, a very large loss. It genuinely feels like the death of the family structure that the child has known for her entire life. Predicting the reaction of adolescents at the initial stage of divorce is similar to predicting the initial reactions to an unexpected death of a loved one. Parents may encounter denial or even pretending that the divorce will soon go away. They may be confronted with anger, hysteria, withdrawal, depression, or deep sadness. The reactions will often develop and transform into other emotional or behavioral states as the children and adolescents move through the process of accepting the loss. Like a death, it is important for parents not to judge or negate the teenager's feelings or reactions. Many adolescents try to talk their parents out of divorce or try to delay their parent's decision in order to avoid the subsequent disruptions and or the strong negative emotions associated with such a great loss.

Children and adolescents commonly blame themselves for their parents' divorce. Youngsters are self-absorbed with a limited perspective on the world. They often are the focus of fights prior to separation and divorce and it is understandable that they would logically see themselves as significant factors in their parents' problems and conflicts. If not for them, they think, their parents might not fight.

For example, Janice was referred to the practice because her grades were suffering, and she was crying at night and withdrawing from friends and family. Her parents were in the process of getting a divorce. During initial office visits, Janice described her parent's divorce and stated that it was all her fault. She had heard her parents argue about her sister and her, and she believed that if she and her sister weren't around to cause the conflict, their parents wouldn't be splitting apart. She regretting not being better behaved or requiring the amount of attention that she asked of her parents. She even recalled that her parents had told her and her sister they weren't to blame for the divorce. This was a 'sure sign' that she must be at fault, she believed, or why would her parents have brought the subject up? We subsequently had several visits with her parents to explain what had happened in the marriage to cause the divorce and that, in fact, Janice and her sister did not cause it.

We often recommend therapy for families to soften some of the harsher consequences of a divorce. Remember, this is a difficult time for adolescents in general. Teenage girls are particularly vulnerable or susceptible to these stressors at this stage. One common pattern is for them to become overly nurturing and protective of the parent. Despite how gratifying this can feel to the parent (who doesn't like to feel loved and cared for?), it represents a breakdown in the parent-child hierarchy. In many ways, this hierarchy is more important in divorced families than in nondivorced families. Such a breakdown can inadvertently allow the teenager too little supervision and too much freedom; responsibility and freedom that they are not yet ready to assume.

Divorce is stressful on everyone in a family and should be viewed by parents as a series of new risks for their children. Longitudinal research indicates that most children come out unscathed in the long term, but more stressed in the first few years. Children from high-conflict divorces or families where parents fail to refocus on their children's needs do not fare as well in the short run and have the risk of more long term problems as adults.

A United Front: Co-Parenting

Parents are divorcing one another, but they are hopefully not divorcing their children. You will always be a mother or father, even after you and your spouse are not husband and wife. The chances that children will positively adjust to a divorce increase dramatically when parents remain involved, parent together, maintain a traditional hierarchy, and demonstrate respect for each other and their children. If a spouse remarries or gains a significant other, that respect should be transferred to this other adult as well. Research data demonstrates a more positive postdivorce outcome for children and adolescents when adults in their lives communicate often and respectfully to one another (Hetherington & Kelly, 2003). They shouldn't bash and trash each other; rather, they need to commit to forming a united parenting front (sometimes with the help of professionals) and keep consistent contact with their children. For divorced parents, striving to establish a high level of communication is essential to their children's long-term welfare.

As stated earlier, some situations develop into complex and contentious family situations. Examples of these include either parent's attempt to explain the causes of the divorce, constructive criticism of the other parent or their parenting style, or even a systematic attempt to alienate the teenager from one parent. Often these more complicated situations require other specific guidelines and strategies, and sometimes, in the situation of alienation, extensive professional help.

In his book, *Divorce Poison* (Regan Books, 2003), Dr. Richard Warshak suggests a five-question test to help determine how a parent should react in these more complicated situations, and it can be useful to instill thought and care into your decisions. These situations usually occur when communication is strained.

1. What is the most honest reason for revealing this information to the children?

2. Are my children apt to be harmed by the behavior I am about to criticize? Can they be harmed by nondisclosure of this information?

3. How will it help the children to hear what I am about to tell them?

4. Do the benefits of telling them outweigh the possible risks?

5. If I was still happily married to my spouse, and I wanted to protect our children's relationships with him or her, how would I handle the situation? (p. 17-18)

It can be easy to rationalize saying negative things to our children with the thought that we are helping them to truly understand the other spouse: "I'm only telling them the truth, it's real. I'm not going to lie to my kids. They have the right to know." Another common pattern is the use of humor to "make light fun" of the ex-spouse. The denigrated spouse becomes the brunt of jokes, sarcasm, or nonverbal innuendo (rolled eyes, facial reaction, etc.) This has the potential to be extremely harmful too, creating lasting damage. In addition to everything else, it is in every child or adolescent's best interest to have an opportunity to develop a good, strong, loving relationship with both parents, and it is every parent's duty to try and facilitate and support this. If nothing else, our teenagers deserve the luxury of having the perception (even if it is untrue) that both their parents are loving and caring, at least until they themselves decide to form their own realistic and more mature relationships with their parents. If you are in doubt about what to do or say concerning the other parent, consult a truly objective friend or a professional before taking action. Remember, bashing another parent can backfire or set in motion long lasting harm to your children. Badmouthing the other parent is badmouthing the child's heritage, which can be detrimental to your teenager's own self-esteem. In addition, undercutting the other parent can often push your teenager to become defensive of the criticized parent and end up hurting your own relationship with your son or daughter in the long run.

A helpful concept is to imagine that a good friend of your son or daughter's is visiting your house. Would you ever make negative comments, verbal or nonverbal, concerning that child's mother or father? What do you suppose that child's reaction would be if you made such a comment? How would this make your child feel if they heard you denigrate their friend's parent?

Introducing a Significant Other

Adolescents have a particular difficulty with adjustment after a divorce in their families. Their lives are already moving at an extremely rapid pace with transition upon transition. Strong peer influences, entering high school, rapid body changes, sexual issues, drug and alcohol influences, emotional and behavioral upheaval (drama) with their friends, higher education choices, impending separation and emancipation from their parents are only some of these stressors. Divorce substantially complicates and compounds these factors.

Current research indicates that Juvenile Service referrals double for adolescents from divorced parents (Hetherington, 2001). Substance abuse occurs at twice the normal rate for this population. Recently, studies have found that these statistics significantly increased when a stepparent or significant other is introduced into teenager's life. Clearly, this increases the stressors and adds further complications and additional adjustments into teenagers' lives. Although a new relationship may bring you joy and comfort, be aware that this same relationship can be very difficult for your children, especially adolescents.

For example, Robbie's world has gone upside down. He's completing his first year in high school and has trouble focusing on his schoolwork. He has had several behavior-related referrals at school. His parents divorced four years ago; his mother remarried two years ago, and his father became engaged this summer. Robbie has had to adjust to a life he could not have imagined. His stepfather is much stricter than his mother is, and Robbie resents the new rules. He wants to become more independent while in high school but instead, he's being more restricted. His father started spending less time with Robbie as he entered high school and now is even more preoccupied with his fiancée and her family. His friends are going out more and dating while he's spending more time at home, grounded because of his grades and behavior. His attitude is surly and he's become sarcastic and cynical. When he came to our office for an evaluation, he obviously was very angry and resented having to see a "shrink." He stated that his parents had more problems than he did. Robbie has been hit and knocked down by multiple stressors that can overwhelm an adolescent at a time when life is already complex. He has been put in a position where he is forced to manage several family and individual issues that he is neither prepared nor properly supported to handle. It is not surprising that he is sneaking alcohol and starting to act out and rebel at home. His reactions are statements of helplessness and frustration.

We urge parents to handle the introduction of a new adult into postdivorce life very carefully, particularly when they have preadolescent or adolescent children. Beyond the profoundly complex developmental stressors in their lives, they are now required to adjust to a complete new set of stressors. Will they like or respect the new adult figure in their lives? Will they feel the competition from two mothers? How will they handle a new parental authority? How will they handle the inevitable loss of attention when their parent focuses on another person? These are just a few of the potential stressors that they may experience. No wonder the resultant behavioral problems increase when parents begin to reconnect with a new relationship.

Many times, adolescents don't express these pressures and frustrations to their parent. Teens have mentioned to us that they don't want to make a parent "unhappy" when they have these negative feelings. They clearly see their parents' happiness after the sadness and stress of the divorce and family breakup, and they often don't want to do or say anything to interfere with this happiness. As a result, teenagers may look elsewhere for ways to express and cope with their frustrations. Adolescents may divert their attentions to a peer group or a significant other of their own. Often this is in reaction to stress and loneliness rather than readiness for a healthy young adult relationship Hetherington's (2003) research found that girls and boys from postdivorce families separated from their parents earlier, often into higher-risk relationships or situations. Parents reported that these separations were often premature.

How are parents best to handle a new significant other in their life? Again, some clear guidelines seem to help in allowing your teenager to effectively cope with another transition. Gradually and directly introduce the idea of you dating. As the relationship develops, communicate clearly and directly with your teen about the relationship and your future plans.

You are the primary parent and your ex-spouse is the co-parent. At first your significant other may feel like an outsider to your adolescent. This is okay; in fact, it is to be expected. At this point, this new significant other is at the same point in the family hierarchy as a babysitter, an uncle, or a grandparent. The significant other is an authority figure who must be treated with respect, and when Mom or Dad is not available (whether he or she is at the store or in the bathroom) the significant other is the authority and should be listened to. When Mom or Dad returns, however, he or she resumes the role of primary authority figure. Simply put, a parent and her new significant other are not (and should not be) on the same level in the family hierarchy. Let the trust and respect build between your teenager and the new adult in his or her life. Let them develop their own relationship, and let this new adult earn his or her status and authority with your teen. This holds true whether you are introducing a new significant other or a stepparent.

You and your ex-spouse have been part of your teen's life for as long as she can remember. It is not realistic to expect her to accept your new significant other immediately, or even soon. Your teenager may resent a new authority, feel that she is betraying the other parent, or just not like this adult chosen by you. If you force the issue, this can lead to problems such as anger, withdrawal, and acting out. Try to incorporate this new adult into your parenting team. We've seen many instances when this can strengthen the support system of your family and not necessarily become another major stressor. We also see that it takes adolescents years of adjustment and work to negotiate all the emotional and relationship obstacles encountered by this new person in their life.

It's safer to go slow—both for you and for the adjustment of your teenager. Don't expect an instant relationship between your new significant other and your teenager just because you like this person. Still, your teenager should treat all adults with respect. Talk out problems if your teen displays unhealthy behavior or disrespect. Start talking individually with your teen and gradually begin to include your significant other into those discussions.

John's parents divorced several years ago and he was referred to the practice because of school problems (attendance, grades, disrespect to teachers). John's mother recently married Sam, a 16-year police veteran. Sam had raised two boys (who were in their twenties at this point) and he thought that John had parents who were too lenient toward him. Sam asserted his opinion about structure and discipline to John's mother and urged her to become more strict and vigilant. John reacted with anger, distrust toward his mom, disrespect towards his parents and teachers. He began failing in school and his parents suspected he was smoking marijuana with some new friends.

John is dealing with one more change that greatly affects his daily life. He resents Sam's stronger authority at a time when he's trying to be more independent and to make his own decisions and mistakes. He did not ask for a new dad; one was thrust upon him, and in fact, Sam has changed John's relationship with his mother, with whom he had been close prior to her remarriage.

Our strategy was to meet with this family and have all the parents agree to a consistent plan to support John in improving his grades. The plan was communicated by his biological parents and supported by Sam. The plan included monitoring and continued communication between parents, teachers, John, and the therapist. When John saw all of the adults being consistent and understanding his needs, he quickly calmed his attitude and focused on his issues.

Of course, along with a new marriage, stepchildren may be part of the mix. Remarrying when one or more party has adolescent children is especially difficult because of an adolescent's developmental agenda; adding new siblings brings further adjustments and stressors. Integrating two families and maintaining a co-parenting relationship with an ex-partner can be challenging. Disagreements, insecurities, miscommunications are a normal part of early stepfamily existence. It is wise to go slowly in establishing close relationships with new family members, and adults should remember to support the family's hierarchy. Firm parenting with compassion benefits all family members. For example, one father we see eliminated the term "step" from "stepchild" and clearly stated that all of the families' children were sons and daughters, not his stepchildren; steps, he said, are something you walk on.

Summary

Parenting children into adulthood is a very difficult job for intact families, much less conflict-laden divorced families. No one handles each situation perfectly or goes through this process without problems. Tolerance and patience are critical skills for dealing with the inevitable family conflicts. It is vital that parents and other family members avoid blaming and scapegoating. Don't take sides or form hostile alliances. Be flexible and communicate through problems rather than ignoring or avoiding them, or generating more conflict. If everyone works together, more parents who care about their family members can translate into more creative ideas and strategies to problem solve. If the adults compromise, negotiate, and seek solutions, this will often generate better parenting strategies. It's important to be encouraging and to be positive to both your children and the other significant adults in the family. This optimism will tend to mobilize other family members to fall in line and raise healthy children and adolescents.

SECTION FOUR

Extreme Environments

CHAPTER 10

Just Leave Me Alone . . . I'm Fine!

Teenage Depression

Steven is a senior in high school. He is intelligent and had always done well in school, but now he is in danger of failing. He can't get out of bed in the morning and is missing classes at an alarming rate. He can't do his homework and is withdrawing from his friends. He used to be a very active, outgoing young man. Now, he almost never sees his friends and his only social contact seems to be via e-mail and instant messages on the computer. He stays awake till all hours of the night and appears to have shut down. His parents suspect that he is drinking, and maybe even starting to use pot.

Unfortunately, scenes like the one described above are not all that unusual for today's teenagers. Steven is depressed. This seems painfully clear. But what do we mean when we say "depressed"? Don't most teenagers feel sad, upset, or depressed at times? What is depression, and how can parents identify depression in their teen? How do you distinguish depression from the normal angst and anxiety of being a teenager? And most importantly, what can you do about it?

When most people use the word "depressed" they are referring to feelings of being sad, blue, down in the dumps, or dysphoric. These are subjective feelings, moods, and emotions. When the word depression is used clinically as a diagnosis, however, it means much more. Depression, in this sense, is an entire syndrome, a cluster of symptoms that typically occur together. Although sadness is one of these individual symptoms, it by itself does not constitute depression. According to the American Psychiatric Association (1994), depression also includes: becoming easily tired or fatigued and having a lack of energy; losing interest in activities that used to be enjoyable and interesting; changes in eating habits (either eating more than usual or less than usual); an increase or a decrease in weight; changes in sleeping habits (difficulty waking up in the morning and sleeping more than normal, difficulty falling asleep at night and sleeping less than normal); feeling worthless or guilty; difficulty concentrating or focusing one's attention; having recurrent thoughts about death or hurting oneself. In general, depression has an impact on a person's mood, the way in which they think, and their activities and behaviors.

Rather than talking about depression as though it is a single, discrete disorder, it really makes more sense to talk about several different forms or types of depressions that exist on a continuum. Some may be very severe, to the point where the individual is a danger to herself; some are less severe. Some types may have a longer duration, some shorter. Some depressions may manifest themselves predominantly through certain specific symptoms or clusters of symptoms, (such as having very little energy, increased appetite, and withdrawal) and some may manifest themselves through others (anxiety, agitation, difficulty sitting still). Some forms of depression may include other, psychotic symptoms, such as hallucinations (hearing or seeing things that do not exist) or delusions (irrational beliefs). Some forms of depression may be very acute (may occur suddenly and without warning) or may develop slowly over time.

Talking about a depressive spectrum, rather than one singular entity, helps to explain why depression is often quite different from one person to another. This also helps to explain why different interventions, even different medications, are often more helpful for some people than for others. Patients and their families often ask us what causes depression. And again, there is not just one simple answer that applies to all cases of depression. Sometimes, there is a clear environmental or psychological cause of depression, such as the death of a loved one. Other times, the individual has no idea what is depressing them; they experience mostly vegetative signs of depression (lack of energy, lack of motivation, increased sleep, increased appetite, withdrawal) and it appears likely that there is a biological or genetic reason for their depression. In most cases, it is probably a combination of the two. One model of depression suggests that individuals can tolerate a certain amount of environmental stress before falling into a depression. The amount of stress an individual is able to withstand is predetermined by his or her biological makeup and genetic background.

One very important point to remember is that depression looks very different in children, adolescents, and adults. The way that people experience depression, and the way in which they express it (whether through their actions, attitudes or feelings) changes over time. A depressed child may cry, a depressed teenager may have a short fuse and get into fights with his parents, a depressed adult may withdraw or start drinking. In fact, the same depressed individual may manifest her depression in all of these ways at different times in her life. Thus, the underlying cause or underlying problem (depression) may be the same, but the overt symptoms may vary from one developmental stage to the next. The technical term for this is *heterotypic continuity*.

The list of depressive symptoms listed above from the American Psychiatric Association is a list of depressive symptoms for adults. These may or may not apply to teenagers who are depressed. For example, for an adult to be depressed, they must experience sadness or a markedly decreased interest in things they used to enjoy. For a teenager to be diagnosed as being depressed, however, they don't necessarily have to experience subjective feelings of sadness. Rather, the emotion that many depressed teenagers experience and express is anger or irritability. Now, of course, teens have a general tendency to be somewhat moody. How many adolescents have you met who were not irritable? But what is the difference between typical, expected moodiness in a teenager and something that we can diagnose as depression? When does it stop being typical and become a disorder? By the same token, most 2-year-olds cry relatively frequently (an expression of sadness) and often have difficulty sleeping through the night. Does this mean that most 2-year-olds are depressed? (Perhaps the more important question is, are most parents of 2-year-olds depressed?)

To answer these questions, we must remember that depression, like any disorder, is more than a simple list of symptoms. First of all, we must look at the extent or the severity of these symptoms and whether they are significantly different from what most other individuals at the same developmental stage, in the same circumstances, would experience. Although a toddler is certainly sad, angry, and upset when she cries, it is not unusual or unnatural for toddlers in general to experience fits of crying (usually regarding bedtime and vegetables). When an adult loses a parent, it is expected that he will feel somewhat sad and lonely and may, for a short time, have difficulty eating or sleeping. Yet, despite the genuine pain that he is experiencing, this is not unusual and would not be considered a disorder. If these reactions persisted for an extended length of time, say 12 to 15 months, then it could possibly be considered something more complex, potentially a disorder.

Secondly, it is not unusual for many of us to frequently experience one or sometimes even two depressive symptoms. For example, many of us may have insomnia, or may become easily fatigued, and many teenagers may be irritable. But this is very different from experiencing a larger group or cluster of these symptoms at the same time. If a teenager is irritable, he may simply be an irritable teenager. If, however, a teenager is irritable, withdrawn, guilty, has low self-esteem, has very little energy, and sleeps 15 hours each day, then he may be suffering from depression.

Thirdly, for any group of symptoms to constitute a disorder, these symptoms must cause the individual some distress or must interfere with her functioning in some meaningful way. Sigmund Freud once wrote that a disorder interferes with a person's ability to "work and love." Thus, if a teenager has some difficulty sleeping and some difficulty concentrating, but this is not interfering with her performance in school, her relationships with her family, and friends, or her performance on the school basketball team, then she probably should not be diagnosed as having depression. Thus, depressed teenagers differ from a typical teenager in that they are significantly more irritable and moody (or sad) than most other teenagers, they experience an entire group or cluster of depressive symptoms, and these symptoms cause some significant distress or impairment in their lives.

Warning Signs for Depression

As we have mentioned, depression may manifest itself very differently from person to person. It takes on many different forms. This is true for teenagers as well as for adults. Therefore, no single list of symptoms can be truly exhaustive and all encompassing. People are individuals, and thus they express their feelings and anxieties in their own, unique manner. Similarly, one or two "red flags" does not necessarily mean that a given individual is suffering from depression, unless these characteristics represent a larger pattern. Among child psychologists, there is the story of a little girl in New York City who was referred for psychological testing. Her teachers thought she was depressed because this particular girl drew all of her pictures in black. The sun was black, the clouds were black, the birds were black, everything in all of her pictures was black. The psychologist tested her and the testing showed no obvious signs of depression. Finally, the psychologist asked the girl, "why do you draw all your pictures in black?" The girl answered that she sat in last row of the class that by the time the crayon box was passed back to her, black was the only color that was left. One warning sign may not necessarily mean anything. Having said that, the following are some common warning signs that a teenager may be suffering from depression.

Clothing

A teenager's clothing often is a reflection of his personality and the way he is feeling at that particular time. For both teenagers and adults, poor hygiene and an unkempt, messy appearance may indicate depression. This may reflect the fact that the person does not care about himself and indicate a "why bother, anyway?" attitude. For teenagers, this sort of appearance turns other teenagers off; it pushes their peers away and serves to isolate the adolescent. At this age, it is developmentally appropriate for a teenager to be very invested in their friends and group interactions. Anything that undermines this interaction or that isolates a teenager may be cause for concern.

Clothing may reflect an adolescent's mood in other ways. Teens, like many of us, often express their personalities and their moods through their clothing. We dress a certain way when we are feeling happy, and we dress very differently when we are feeling sad or upset. If an adolescent dresses in very dark, black, severe clothing, it may reflect a dark, negative, depressive mood. This may, however, simply be a reflection of a certain personal style. By itself, this tendency probably does not mean much and should not be a cause for concern. If it occurs in conjunction with other behaviors or warning signs, however, it could be a signal that your teenager may be struggling with some form of depression or other serious difficulty.

Music and Other Media

Teens also express their moods and feelings in other ways, aside from how they dress. It is quite common for adolescents to listen to music, and to a lesser extent to watch movies, television shows, and even read books that are in keeping with how they are feeling. Music, especially, helps them to give their feelings a voice, and to express these feelings and frustrations. In many ways, this is extremely healthy and adaptive: it provides an outlet for these and other emotions, so that they do not remain bottled up or expressed in other, more impulsive ways. Certain types of popular music are often associated with sadness and depression, or even anger. Get to know what types of music your teen listens to, and what movies, books, and shows he likes. Aside from helping you ascertain whether your teen is depressed, talking with him about these and other interests shows that you care about him and helps to open the lines of communication.

Self-Harm

One of the most dangerous indicators that an adolescent may be suffering from depression is self-harm, or cutting. Cutting most frequently occurs on the hands, wrist, arms, or legs. Cuts may be serious enough to constitute a suicidal gesture or attempt, or they may be more superficial, and not be intended to cause serious harm. Often, when teenagers cut themselves superficially, they do so in order to "feel something" or "for the sensation." Sometimes, these cuts are intended as a form of self-punishment. Interestingly, some researchers in this area have begun to view this type of cutting as being more similar to alcohol or drug addiction than to a form of suicidal gesture. Regardless, cutting is considered to be a very serious warning sign of depression. Often, teenagers try to hide their scars by wearing long sleeves, or even gloves, in warm weather or at inappropriate times. We have had teenagers come to our office intending to wear gloves inside for an entire session (or long-sleeve shirts in very hot, humid weather) in order to cover up the evidence of their self-harm.

Social Isolation

It is very natural for teenagers to be social and to be extremely concerned, almost preoccupied, with their peers and social interactions. This investment, when channeled effectively, is healthy and developmentally appropriate. It is therefore somewhat worrisome for teens to withdraw and isolate themselves from social interaction. This is especially true if such withdrawal constitutes a change from their usual pattern of interacting with others and if they stop taking part in activities that they normally enjoy. This could include not going over friends' houses, quitting a club or sports team, or not being as active socially on the weekends. One potential warning sign of this withdrawal is a teen's increased reliance on e-mail and the Internet for social interactions, especially if she used to be more outgoing. Now, let us be clear about this: using the Internet does not make a person depressed (unless they have a really slow modem). An increased reliance on this form of communication, however, or using this as the primary form of communication, may help a teenager insulate herself from more direct social interactions. This insulation, and the reasons that underlie it, are the possible indicators of loneliness and depression, not the use and enjoyment of the Internet itself.

Behavior Changes

As we discussed earlier, depression, by definition, is a change in someone's ongoing, stable personality. As such, depression is often accompanied by other changes in an adolescent's behavior. Any significant change in behavior, attitude, or general functioning that cannot reasonably be attributed to other factors could be a warning sign of depression. Possibly the most common changes that are associated with depression include a marked drop in grades or poor school attendance. Similarly, starting to use substances (drugs, alcohol or nicotine) or a sharp increase in the use of these substances may also indicate depression. Often, when we talk with teenagers who are struggling with depression or other difficulties, they say that they drink, smoke, or use drugs as a means of feeling better or getting away from what upsets them. In these cases, it is not only necessary to treat not simply the symptom, the drug or alcohol use (and replace it with more adaptive ways of coping), but the underlying depression as well. Finally, sudden changes in friendships or relationships are often associated with depression. Losing these types of relationships not only may indicate depression but may also trigger or contribute to it.

Emotional Indicators

Teenagers are often very moody when depressed. Their feelings tend to change very quickly, and often for no apparent reason. Small, seemingly inconsequential things will set them off, causing them to become angry, resentful, sad, or withdrawn. As we noted earlier, teenagers do not need to be sad to be clinically depressed. They can simply be irritable. For example, Susan was brought into therapy because of angry, violent behaviors. She would appear calm and happy one minute and then, according to her parents, become furious and aggressive the next. Often, it turned out, these episodes were in response to what she felt was criticism from her father or from her friends. She said that she was trying to control her temper, but that she just couldn't. And the more her parents and her psychologist worked with her to control her behavior, the angrier she became. Finally, her psychologist and her parents tried a different approach. Although she never reported feeling sad, they decided that Susan should see a psychiatrist and be evaluated for antidepressant medication. Also at this time, Susan and her psychologist stopped talking about her behavior and her anger, and, instead, focused on other feelings: loneliness, feeling isolated and not fitting in, not living up to her parents' expectations. As she began to take the medication, it became easier to talk about these topics. Although it was no longer a topic in therapy, Susan's anger and violent outbursts began to subside. She never reported feeling sad, but it turned out that she was depressed. She simply never recognized this, or realized that this was driving her anger and frustration.

When talking with teens about their moods or emotions, we are often tempted to ask *why*. "Why are you feeling this way? Why are you upset?" Usually, we receive responses like "because" or "I don't know" or a flat denial, like "I'm not angry" (or sad, or so on). Chances are, if teens could answer, they would. But usually, they genuinely do not know why they are angry, sad, or upset. They just are. And "I don't know" may often be a legitimate answer.

Some teenagers, when depressed, feel the opposite of being irritable and become more passive. They stop asserting themselves and pushing for increased independence. For example, they may say that it is no big deal if they do not get their driver's license. It is natural for teenagers to strive towards adulthood and independence. They provide the energy, the impetus, for the eventual separation between parents and adolescents. Part of this process is learning how to assert oneself effectively and appropriately. If this is not the case, then it may indicate that something is wrong.

Similarly, it is healthy and natural for teenagers to be very future oriented. Their entire life is ahead of them (or so it seems) and they tend to focus on what is in store for them. This is healthy and adaptive. If they are not looking forward to future events and milestones, then this, too, may indicate depression.

Another way to determine if your teen is feeling depressed is to use yourself as a barometer of how they are feeling. As we have noted, in families, we are often made to feel the way others are feeling. This is more than simply empathizing with others or being sensitive to what they are feeling. Family members, especially teenagers, actually induce feelings and emotions in the rest of us. This is not done on purpose or (only) in a manipulative fashion. It is just the way families work. Thus, if you, the parent start to feel depressed, and you are not sure why, it may be an indication that your teenager is feeling depressed.

Teenagers, like all of us, often look for ways to express their feelings. This is a very healthy and adaptive strategy, which helps us to better understand our feelings and helps to make them less intimidating and overwhelming. It is not uncommon for teenagers to express their feelings, including sadness and depression, in their artwork. We have had adolescent patients who have written poetry describing their depression, written screenplays examining why they are depressed, and have taken photographs or done drawings or paintings that graphically illustrated their plight. If your teen shows you her artwork, and it contains a depressive theme, don't be afraid to point it out and to discuss it with her. Chances are she is showing this to you for a reason. She may not know how else to broach the subject.

Often, regression can be a warning sign of depression. In this sense, regression does not have to mean that your teenage son dives on the floor in a fetal position and begins sucking his thumb. Rather, regression could simply be opening up and returning to old topics and issues that you thought had already been resolved. For example, it is your sixteen year-old daughter's job to take out the trash. She used to resist and argue that this wasn't fair and that she didn't want to do it. With a lot of hard work and exceptional parenting, you were able to resolve this issue and she has been cheerfully taking the trash out after dinner for the entire semester. Suddenly, she begins complaining about taking the trash out again. Returning to an old, previously resolved issue could indicate that your teenager is feeling anxious, under stress, and possibly depressed.

Finally, repeated, ritualistic behaviors may be a warning sign for depression. This may include hair or hand washing, needing to arrange things (books, pencils, clothes) in a certain manner, repeatedly standing up and sitting down, turning lights and electrical appliances on and off, or repeatedly counting things. These behaviors may indicate anxiety and what is called *agitated depression*.

Warning Signs of Teenage Depression: Summary

- *Severe withdrawal.* More than simply not talking with parents, watch for a teen who is closing himself off from all friends and family members; isolating himself in his room and having less contact with others overall.

- *Change in appearance.* Pay attention to a teen who has poor hygiene or a lack of concern about her appearance, or whose clothing or hair appears unkempt or disheveled.

- *Clothing:* A teen may start constantly wearing very dark, black, or "depressed-looking" outfits and makeup as more than a fashion statement.

- *Wearing long-sleeves or gloves at inappropriate or unnecessary times:* This may be an attempt to cover up cuts, slashes, or burns.

- *An increase in e-mail use, Internet use, or other means of indirect contact:* Teens may use such methods of communication to as a way to withdraw and relate with others in more limited, less immediately connected fashion.

- *A change in musical tastes:* Teens may suddenly have an affinity for music that is associated with depressive themes and/or suicide.

- *Commencement of or increase in drug or alcohol use.*

- *Any significant change in likes, dislikes, habits, or personality.*

- *Increased anger and/or irritability.*

- *You, the parent, begin to feel run down or depressed.*

- *Cuts, slashes, bruises, or burns*: These are often found on the wrists, arms, and legs but could appear on other parts of the body as well.

- *Loss of interest in activities or hobbies that they used to find enjoyable:* These may include music, sports, socializing with friends. This is especially true for more physically active pursuits.

- *Increased passivity*: Depressed teens may cease to assert themselves to parents and peers, allowing others to "run over" them.

- *Decreased academic performance.*

- *Lack of interest in future plans and events*: Teens may appear not to be looking forward to anything at all.

- *Increased moodiness and irritability*: A depressed teen may experience sudden mood changes, for no apparent reason and with little provocation.

- *Negative emotions expressed creatively:* Teens may express sadness, hopelessness, isolation, or anger in their writing or artwork.

- *Poor school attendance*: This symptom may include missing school or tardiness.

- *Arriving late to other activities in addition to school.*

- *Changing friends, or a pattern of changing friends*: Depressed teens may have difficulty maintain long-term relationships.

- *Regression:* Teens may begin to repeating behaviors or re-visit issues from the past.

- *Repeated, ritualistic behaviors.*

What Parents Can Do to Help a Depressed Teen

Okay, so now that you can identify whether your teen may be suffering from depression, what can you do to help him cope with his sadness, with-drawal, isolation, and irritability? Although ultimately, your teen must work to help himself, some general strategies and approaches will allow you to support your teen.

Before we discuss what parents can do to help, we would like to state one thing very clearly: this does not imply that parents have caused their son or daughter to become depressed. As we mentioned earlier, many, many different factors contribute to depression. The behaviors of the parents or the family may or may not be one such factor for any given teenager. Regardless of which factors underlie the depression, parents are still one of the most powerful resources an adolescent can possibly have in the fight to overcome depression. Even if parents are not the problem, they can certainly be a large part of the solution.

The first way in which parents can help is by making sure that the structure, integrity, and hierarchy of the family remains intact. The family is the context and structure in which children and teenagers develop. It provides grounding and support, and models for the teen how people interact with each other, communicate, and cope with fears, frustrations, and anger. Making sure the family structure is intact provides support and an atmosphere where teens can work out many of their problems. Earlier in the book, we discussed the basic principles of attachment theory; it is certainly true that all of us are better able to cope with the normal pressures of life if we have a secure base and grounding at home.

A teenager's depression can easily affect the family structure. In fact, when the natural family order becomes twisted in these cases, it may serve to support and even enable an adolescent's depression. The fact that a teenager is depressed does not change the basic definition and structure of a healthy family, a family where the parents still set the tone and are in charge. Parents should never feel that they are constrained in their interactions with their teen or that they need to walk on eggshells. They must feel comfortable and confident enough to do what they think is right.

By retaining control of the family, parents accomplish several goals. First, they set themselves up as strong, capable individuals, worthy adversaries against whom their teens may push (see Chapter 3). Similarly, they convey the view that the teen is not weak or defective. We are certainly not advocating being mean or unsympathetic to an adolescent who is undoubtedly experiencing a great deal of pain. But if parents treat their depressed adolescents as though they are fragile and unable to cope with their depression, teens will start to believe this of themselves. Allowing one family member's depression to become the central focus of a family can give rise to a family structure that reinforces that depression. Rather, the goal should be to maintain a healthy, balanced family hierarchy that, in time, will support and help the teenager cope with his or her difficulties.

An important warning sign that a teenager's depression is starting to take too much control of a family is when the parents begin to feel and react in ways that they themselves do not feel are right. As we mentioned previously, a depressed teenager will often make parents feel and act depressed. In this way, whole families may become depressed and reinforce each other's anxieties and frustrations. In a similar vein, when teens are depressed, they expect us to react to them in certain ways—with anger or frustration, for example. It can be quite difficult to stop ourselves from being drawn in to these self-fulfilling prophecies and thereby supporting and fueling their depression.

Donna had been depressed for some time, and her mother was losing patience and hope. After many weeks of trying (and being rebuffed), she stopped offering to drive Donna places and encouraging Donna to go out with her friends. She stopped asking Donna about her homework. When medication and therapy began to help, Donna started to improve, or so it seemed to her psychologist. But Donna's mother did not see this improvement; she still saw the same patterns that had been there for weeks. It turned out that Donna's mother was still treating her as though she were depressed. She said wouldn't ask Donna to do things because she didn't want to "open a can of worms and get her and everybody else upset." Similarly, Donna reported that she wouldn't ask her mother for rides because it always seemed that her mother was angry at her and that it seemed that she didn't want to take her anywhere. She said her mother didn't care about her because she would never help her with her homework. It felt like her mother didn't think she could do it, and that she was a disappointment to her mother. Donna began to feel that her mother was depressed, that whenever she saw her mother, she seemed sad, sullen, and frustrated, and this exacerbated Donna's own emotions.

In addition to all the things that parents can do on their own at home, sometimes it is still helpful to seek professional help and guidance. First and foremost, it is vital to determine if there is a physical cause for your teenager's symptoms, such as hypothyroidism or anemia. Your internist, pediatrician, or family practitioner can help with this. After these physical causes have been ruled out, the next step is to see a qualified mental health professional, such as a psychologist, psychiatrist, or clinical social worker, for a formal diagnosis.

If a professional diagnoses your teen with a clinical depression, the research clearly and consistently shows that a combination of medication and therapy is the best and most efficient treatment. Medication can be very helpful in treating many of the symptoms of depression. This is especially true for a group of symptoms that are sometimes referred to as *vegetative* or *endogenous*. These symptoms include increased need for sleep, a lack of energy, increased appetite or weight gain, and difficulty concentrating. In this sense, taking an antidepressant for these symptoms is just like having the flu and taking aspirin for the fever and headaches. Therapy, however, is somewhat different. Therapy does not necessarily target specific symptoms the way medication does; rather, it helps the teenager make long-term changes and adjustments in how they look at themselves and how they cope with the world around them. Therapy can help a teen develop a more positive sense of themselves, feel less dependent and more secure in their relationships with others, and create strategies for coping with frustration and for expressing this frustration in a constructive and verbal manner. Medication can makes it easier for the teenager to do what is required in therapy to produce long-term changes and resolutions.

Parents frequently ask us how to convince their teenager to enter therapy in the first place. At times, this is no easy task. Sometimes, however, it is simply a matter of finding a psychologist, social worker or counselor who is the right fit for this particular teenager. There are many competent therapists out there, but not everyone is the right fit for every patient. If the professional is a good fit, chances are that the teenager will agree to treatment; if the therapeutic relationship is not a good fit and the teen resists, treatment with that professional probably would not be very helpful in the first place.

Other strategies include offering your teenager alternatives to standard individual therapy. These options include family therapy or group therapy. Family therapy focuses not just on the presenting problem (the teenager's depression) but also on the communication patterns, connections and relationships within the family. It will often focus very concretely on what the family as a whole can do to improve the situation. Family therapy can be useful because it helps to take the pressure and the focus off the teenager. Rather than being made to feel that it everything is the teenager's fault and that they are the problem, entering family therapy very openly and overtly states that there are issues and problems that reside within the family as a whole, not just in one person. No one person is responsible; everyone is equally responsible. A second option is group therapy. In group therapy, teenagers come to session with other teens, more or less the same age as themselves. Others in the group may have very similar concerns; some may be working on different issues. Group therapy is conducted in a very similar fashion to individual therapy, but with several people in the room. Not only do teenagers have the opportunity to discuss themselves and their own lives but to hear how others do the same. They give feedback and advice to each other. It is very therapeutic for a teenager to be in the position of helping someone else. Further, your teen may give more credence to advice from another teenager than to the same advice from an adult. Groups are very natural setting for a teenager. At this developmental level, they are very social creatures. To teens, group therapy feels natural, comfortable and, when successful, incredibly secure. Interestingly, advice from other group members in sessions is often more direct and to the point than what the therapist would say.

Suicide: A Parent's Worst Fear

By far, the most serious symptom or by-product of depression is suicide. It can be frightening even to talk about it. Females are much more likely than males to attempt suicide, but males are more likely than females to actually kill themselves. Warning signs of suicide include having a specific plan for harming themselves, a history of past *suicide attempts* (actually trying to kill themselves) or *suicidal gestures* (hurting or threatening to hurt themselves without actually attempting to kill themselves, such as superficially cutting their arms), or giving away prized possessions or things with strong sentimental meaning. Ironically, a teenager may also be at risk for suicide if he or she has been severely depressed and is now starting to improve. Depressed individuals in this situation may find that they now have more energy and motivation to implement a plan for self-harm than before.

What can parents do if they fear that their teen may be suicidal? The overall answer is anything and everything you can do to protect them, even if they do not want your help. There are some mistakes that teenagers should be allowed to make to learn things for themselves. Obviously, suicide is not one of them. In this case, parents have the responsibility to be safety nets for their teenagers and to protect them.

First of all, take some very clear, concrete precautions to remove the opportunity for self-harm. This includes removing weapons, especially guns, and denying them access to other potentially harmful implements: knives, razors, scissors, tools, and so on. Lock these things up or remove them from your home, regardless of the inconvenience. In addition, do not allow your teenager to be alone. Always have him in your line of sight. Your teen will not like this, but it may be necessary for a period of time. Finally, take your teen to see a professional psychologist, psychiatrist, or social worker. There is no need for parents to take on this responsibility themselves without support.

Sometimes parents are not sure how grave the danger is and which precautions are enough. In these cases, it is better by far to err on the side of caution. If you find yourself lying awake at night in bed worrying if your teenager is going to be safe until the next morning, then be proactive and take her to the emergency room immediately. This serves a number of purposes. First of all, it shows that you are listening to your teenager and that you are taking what she says seriously. In and of itself, this can be very useful. Showing your teen, specifically and concretely, that you are listening and that you care can help her tremendously. Otherwise you run the risk that she will take further steps to show you that she is serious. Even teens who do not truly want to kill themselves sometimes do so anyway, either impulsively or accidentally while trying to make a statement. Taking your teen to the hospital clearly demonstrates that you are listening to her, that you respect her enough to take what she says seriously, and that you care about her. In addition, going to the emergency room is not generally a pleasant experience. It will be long, boring, uncomfortable, and probably embarrassing. This shows your teenager that there are natural consequences for her actions. This is not a punishment, but the natural, logical response to something as serious as a suicide threat.

Finally, try to talk with your adolescent about the future. Help him to see that there will be a time when his current problems will be past him. Committing suicide is a permanent solution to a temporary problem. Help him to be more future oriented and optimistic, to see what his future can be like, and what he will be giving up. Talk with him about his goals, plans, and aspirations. This discussion could address what he wants out of life when he grows up or graduates high school, what he wants to do this summer, or what his plans are for the weekend. Help him to express his fears, anger, and frustrations. The more these feelings are expressed verbally, the less likely it is that these feelings will become manifest through dangerous behaviors.

Having a depressed teen is frustrating and painful for any parent. It is difficult to watch someone you love so much hurt so badly, while at the same time you want to scream, "Just snap out of it!!" You may find yourself wanting to give up in despair. First, remember that it does not have to last a lifetime. With the right support, the right resources and the right interventions, your teenager can and will get through this, and so will you. Secondly, as we have said before, what you do, including making mistakes, is often not as important as the fact that you continue to try time and time again, despite your mistakes. Caring and trying to help, and showing that you care and are trying to help, is often the best intervention of all.

CHAPTER 11

BOUNCING OFF THE WALLS

ADHD

Attention-Deficit/Hyperactivity Disorder, or ADHD, is one of the most overused diagnoses today. According to the American Psychiatric Association, ADHD should be found in only about 3-5% of the population. ADHD is currently diagnosed in children and teenagers at almost twice this rate, however. In some ways, ADHD has become a catchall diagnosis that some physicians and clinicians apply to almost any child or adolescent who is moody, irritable, oppositional or defiant, disrespectful or who has difficulty concentrating in school. Overusing the label ADHD only serves to undermine the legitimacy and benefit of accurately applying this diagnosis. In its own way, ADHD may be as pervasive and debilitating as autism.

What is ADHD?

ADHD does not mean "a child who misbehaves in school." Rather, ADHD is a very specific diagnosis with very specific symptoms, which are listed in Table 12–1. As can be seen, these symptoms may be organized into three major groups: those having to do with inattention, those that pertain to hyperactivity, and those that indicate impulsivity. These are the hallmarks of the disorder. Prior to 1994, the American Psychiatric Association recognized two separate diagnoses, Attention-Deficit Disorder (ADD) with hyperactivity, and ADD without hyperactivity. In 1994, the Association combined these two disorders into one, ADHD, with three

TABLE 12-1: DSM-IV Criteria for Attention-Deficit/Hyperactivity Disorder

A. Either (1) or (2)

   1. six or more of the following symptoms of inattention have persisted for at least 6 months to a degree that is maladaptive and inconsistent with developmental level
   a. often fails to give close attention to details or makes careless mistakes
   b. often has difficulty sustaining attention
   c. often does not seem to listen when spoken to directly
   d. often does not follow through on instructions and fails to finish school work, chores or duties in the workplace
   e. often has difficulty organizing tasks and activities
   f. often avoids, dislikes or is reluctant to engage in tasks that require sustained mental effort
   g. often loses things necessary for tasks or activities
   h. is often easily distracted by extraneous stimuli
   i. is often forgetful in daily activities

   2. six or more of the following symptoms of hyperactivity-impulsivity have persisted for at least 6 months to a degree that is maladaptive and inconsistent with developmental level
   a. often fidgets with hands or feet or squirms in seat
   b. often leaves seat in classroom or in other situation in which remaining seated is expected
   c. often runs about or climbs excessively in situations in which it is inappropriate
   d. often has difficulty playing or engaging
   e. is often "on the go" or often acts as if "driven by a motor"
   f. often talks excessively
   g. often blurts out answers before questions have been completed
   h. often has difficulty waiting turn
   i. often interrupts or intrudes

B. Some symptoms were present before age 7 years.

C. Some impairment from the symptoms is present in two or more setting

D. There must be clear evidence of clinically significant impairment in social, academic or occupational functioning.

E. The symptoms are not better accounted for by another clinical disorder

Source: American Psychiatric Association (1994) p. 83-85.

recognized subtypes: primarily inattentive, primarily hyperactive, or combined. (Don't ask why they changed this; it's a mystery.) Thus, one individual may be diagnosed with ADHD and not be hyperactive, and another with the same diagnosis may have no difficulty focusing and controlling his attention.

According to the American Psychiatric Association, ADHD is four to nine times more common in males than in females. It is unclear, however, if these numbers indicate that ADHD is actually more common in males than in females, or if it simply more commonly reported and formally diagnosed in males than in females. As we've noted, where boys tend to act *out* and are more likely to be diagnosed with things like conduct disorder or oppositional-defiant disorder, girls keep things *in* and are more predisposed to things like depression. It is possible that boys with ADHD are simply louder and exhibit more behavioral difficulties (particularly in school) and therefore receive a diagnosis and treatment. Girls, however, may be inattentive and have trouble focusing, but do not act out and cause problems and therefore go unnoticed and slip through the cracks. The squeaky wheel gets the grease, or in this case, the diagnosis and the Ritalin.

Never the Same Thing Twice

One of the patterns we have found with ADHD is that, even in the same person, the symptoms can be highly variable. What this means is that on any given day, an individual with ADHD may be able to concentrate, sit still for long periods of time, and control his impulsivity. This same person may have a great deal of difficulty performing the same behaviors and completing the same tasks the next day. Thus, Monday in school, John may have no problems paying attention to the teacher, taking notes, and completing his work, the model student. On Tuesday, however, in the same class, with the same teacher covering the same material using the same teaching techniques, John may be distractible, fidgety, and unfocused. He may daydream or talk with his friends and be generally disruptive to the class. Such inconsistency or variability is typical for this particular disorder.

This pattern causes difficulties both for the individual and for teachers and professionals who work with them. Children and teenagers with ADHD seem to perform just well enough to raise everyone else's expectations for them, and then they appear to fall short or fail the very next day. Naturally, parents and professionals attribute this to not trying, not caring, or not being responsible, when in fact this pattern is a natural symptom of their disorder and is probably out of the teen's control. Other disorders, such as some forms of depression or mental retardation elicit caring, support, and sympathy, but this pattern of inconsistency and variability in ADHD elicits negative, almost rejecting reactions from others.

Teenagers with ADHD tend to react to others' frustration and rejection in one of two ways. First, like most of us, teens respond to anger with anger, to rejection with rejection. If this happens often enough, it becomes a pattern. Teens start to expect this rejection. They look for it and assume that this is how they will be treated. Soon, they start to react angrily to teachers and parents, even when there is no criticism. They are then labeled as being disrespectful or oppositional, which reinforces the cycle of rejection in a self-fulfilling prophecy.

Secondly, teens may start to believe that they deserve this rejection and the criticism. They may internalize this view of themselves and come to see themselves as lazy, irresponsible, or bad. This pattern is much more subtle and insidious. This affects their self-esteem and how they see themselves, their potential, and their abilities.

Although a diagnosis of ADHD specifically, concretely refers to difficulties controlling one's impulsivity and hyperactivity, or focusing one's attention, secondary issues often develop from these core symptoms. Issues with self-esteem, insecurity, frustration tolerance, and peer relationships are not specifically part of the diagnosis, but often cause as much difficulty and distress for a teenager as the core symptoms. It is often very useful to address these insecurities and interpersonal issues in addition to whatever interventions are made to address impulsivity and inattention.

The ADHD Diagnosis

This pattern of variability makes it very difficult to reliably diagnose ADHD. On a given day, at any particular time, a child or teen with ADHD will have no significant difficulties with inattention or impulsivity.

Therefore, it would not be very accurate to evaluate a teenager once for one hour, or even three hours, and then assume that this three-hour block of time reflects this teenager's typical behaviors and abilities. To make matters even worse, there is some research to show that working one-on-one with someone, in a quiet, distraction-free setting, in a new or novel environment helps people with ADHD to focus their attention better and control their impulsivity for short periods of time. So it is not just possible but even somewhat probable that a child or teenager with ADHD will not exhibit their ADHD symptoms in a one-time evaluation in a doctor's office.

So how do we assess whether or not someone has ADHD? First of all, it is often very useful to evaluate a teenager's behavior in more than one setting. Rather than just looking at the teenager's behavior in the doctor's office, it is important to get a picture of how they behave at home and in school. This may be done through direct observation (such as visiting the school and observing the classroom) or gathering information from those who see the teenager in these settings on a daily basis. Towards this end, psychologists evaluating a teenager for ADHD often distribute questionnaires to teachers, parents, and the teenager. These questionnaires help the evaluator to form a picture of the adolescent's typical behavior, rather than generalizing from a single observation.

In addition to the questionnaires, it is still useful to conduct some face-to-face testing when assessing someone for ADHD. Most of these tests examine teenagers' memory and their ability to concentrate and focus their attention. Specifically, most of these tests look at something called executive functioning. Executive functioning is the cognitive ability to decide on what you will focus, the ability to allocate mental resources and to choose, "I need to focus on this book," as opposed to your actual *ability* to focus on the book. To put it another way, executive functioning is the ability to regulate and, when needed, inhibit, yourself as opposed to acting upon the world around you. It is this skill that has been implicated in ADHD. In many ways, this makes sense. If a teenager with ADHD was *unable* to focus his attention at all, ever, then we would not see the variability that is typical of the disorder.

Many tests of executive functioning exist. Standard IQ tests, such as the Wechsler Intelligence Scale for Children, Fourth Edition (WISC-IV) or the Wechsler Adult Intelligence Scale, Third Edition (WAIS-III), do not specifically measure executive functioning, however. They do assess short-term memory, and although this is related to executive functioning, it is not quite the same thing. Administered as part of a comprehensive assessment of an individual suspected of having ADHD, an IQ test can provide information about the person's cognitive abilities in general, their strengths and weaknesses, and how they process different types of information. But an IQ test (sometimes called a cognitive test) does not specifically address whether or not a teenager has ADHD: it does not specifically measure executive functioning, and it in no way assesses a teenager's level of hyperactivity or impulsivity. That said, however, ADHD is not simply a deficit in executive functioning. Rather, a diagnosis of ADHD means that such a deficit manifests itself in a way that significantly interferes with the person's overall functioning.

The ADHD Masquerade

Even with a comprehensive evaluation, it is often difficult to differentiate ADHD from other disorders that manifest in very similar ways. For example, a teenager who comes into our office because he is having difficulties in school, can't concentrate on his homework, is distracted during class, irritable, fights with his parents, and appears withdrawn and sullen may have ADHD. The same teenager may also have some form of depression, bipolar disorder, a learning disability, or a crush on his teacher. Trying to determine a diagnosis based on this set of symptoms would be like going to a pediatrician's office and saying that your child has a fever, upset stomach, and a sore throat, and then trying to differentiate among the flu, a cold, allergies, and strep throat.

The symptoms of ADHD are very similar to some forms of depression. For example, difficulty concentrating is listed as a symptom of both major depression and a form of low-level, long lasting depression called dysthymia. And both phases of bipolar disorder (formerly known as manic depression) bear some similarities to ADHD: the depressive phase of bipolar disorder involves difficulty with concentration, and the manic phase is characterized by a decreased need for sleep, being more talkative than usual, and an increase in goal-directed activity, much like the hyperactivity and impulsivity that we see in teenagers with ADHD. In fact, some have suggested that many of the teenagers currently diagnosed with ADHD would be more accurately diagnosed as having bipolar disorder. Another diagnosis that is difficult to differentiate from ADHD is Asperger's Syndrome, a very high-functioning, intelligent, and verbal form of autism. In addition to other features, Asperger's Syndrome is characterized by a lack of interest in social, interpersonal interactions, like an extreme form of aloofness. Many children and teenagers with Asperger's Syndrome are misdiagnosed with ADHD because this lack of interest is misinterpreted as inattention. Finally, distractibility and hyperactivity in school may be the result of anxiety, whether because of a specific learning disability, a lack of confidence in one's intellectual abilities (real or perceived, including some forms of mild mental retardation) or social/interpersonal factors that may be specific to a particular subject or a particular teacher.

Treatments and Interventions for ADHD

Once, a parent came into our office with her teenage son. After listening to her concerns, the psychologist agreed with the teenager's existing diagnosis of ADHD, and proceeded to explain that such and such is typical for ADHD, and this is what the literature says should be done when working with ADHD. As the psychologist talked, the mother's face grew redder and redder, and she became angrier and angrier. Finally, she interrupted the psychologist and said furiously, "My son is not ADHD, he is John!" She said that she did not want to work with someone who going to treat ADHD, she wanted someone who was going to treat her son, John. And she walked out of the office.

She was absolutely right. Whether it is ADHD or another disorder, people are not simply collections of symptoms, labels, and diagnoses. These types of disorders impact all aspects of the individual's life and affect each person uniquely. If we try to treat only the disorder, chances are we will not be successful, and we will only be solving a portion of the puzzle. This is especially true when working with teenagers for whom everything is growing, changing, developing, and interconnected. Having raised this cautionary note, it is also important to realize that the existing research can be extremely useful in formulating an intervention strategy to treat the individual teenager.

Medication

TO MEDICATE OR NOT?

The research clearly indicates that the most effective intervention to help individuals control their inattention is medication. The research also shows, however, that although these medications are very useful in controlling these specific symptoms, they do not cure or correct the underlying problem. Once the individual stops taking these medications, the difficulties with inattention immediately return. Taking these medications can make it easier for the teenager to control, compensate for, or deal with these difficulties, however. Medication can allow a teenager to develop other coping mechanisms, such as improved organizational skills. In this way, medication is a *tool* rather than a crutch. If a crutch is removed, the person using it cannot stand on her own. A tool, however, is something that a person chooses to use or to not use. She is not dependent upon it, but she may choose to use it to make a particular task easier. Without a specific tool, the individual could still probably complete the task through other means, although it might be more difficult. Medication may be useful, but does not have to be something on which the teenager feels dependent. This may simply be a matter of choosing this mindset, but such a mindset can help teenagers feel that they have control over themselves and their lives rather than being powerless. It sets the stage for taking responsibility.

In addition, medication may be helpful in other ways. Assume that an individual has a limited or finite amount of mental energy. Anyone who has ever crammed for a final exam or has stayed up late working on a term paper knows what it is like not to be able to think clearly and effectively anymore. If people do have a limited amount of mental energy, all of us need to use a certain amount of this just to compose ourselves, to listen to what is going on around us, to monitor ourselves, and to make decisions about what we are about to do. If this requires, for example, 25% of our mental energy, then we have 75% of our resources left to make friends, get along with others, to learn long division and how to shoot a jump-shot, among other things. An individual with ADHD may require 40%, 50%, or even 60% of their mental resources, however, just, as one of our patients puts it, "to hold it together." This individual then only has 60%, 50%, or even 40% of their resources left to do all the other things they have to do in his life. As a result, these other things, such as academics or getting along with friends or parents, often suffer. Medication cannot specifically improve peer relations or spelling. It can free up more mental energy, making it possible for the teenager to allot a greater amount of his mental, emotional, and cognitive resources to these areas. As a result, medication often helps teenagers improve in these secondary areas that are not specifically and directly affected by ADHD.

Studies show that about 72% of individuals correctly and rigorously diagnosed with ADHD experience a significant decrease in inattention and impulsivity in response to stimulant medications. But this means that between one-third and one-fourth of people with ADHD will *not* improve when prescribed these medications. Thus, whether or not a teenager responds to these medications should not be used to determine whether or not a teenager has ADHD.

Only a medical doctor or a nurse practitioner can prescribe medications. The medical doctors who are specifically and formally trained in these types of medications are psychiatrists. Many pediatricians, internists, and general practitioners have made it their business to learn about these medications and have become comfortable and experienced in prescribing them, however. When there is a thorough psychological assessment asserting a diagnosis of ADHD, it is often a good first step to go to the teenager's pediatrician or general practitioner for medication. If this professional does not feel comfortable treating ADHD, it would then be wise to ask for a referral to a psychiatrist. Often, after the psychiatrist gets a the teenager set on the right dosage of the right medication, the pediatrician or general practitioner can then do follow-up visits and medication management.

WHAT'S PRESCRIBED AND HOW MUCH?

Stimulants are the class of medications most commonly used to treat ADHD; including Ritalin, Adderall, Concerta, and Dexadrine. Just as one person may take aspirin for a headache and another may respond better to ibuprofen, one teenager may respond very well to Ritalin but not to Dexadrine, while a second teenager could display the exact opposite pattern. Another class of medication that may be effective is similar to antidepressants such as Prozac and Zoloft.

To further complicate matters, even if a teenager is taking the right medication (a medication that potentially could be very effective and help-ful for them), if they are not taking the right dosage, then the medication will not have the desired effect. Too little of the "correct" medication may have almost no effect whatsoever, while too much may make teens overly tired and not improve their attention and concentration at all. Finding the right dosage of the right medication is not an easy task. Different individuals metabolize different medications at different rates, and even though research-based guidelines exist, there are still no hard and fast rules to determine who will respond well to what amount of which medi-cation. Thus, there is a quite a bit of trial and error in medicating an individual with ADHD.

Typically, the psychiatrist will start with a very low dose of Medication A. If this does not produce the desired effect, then he or she will increase the dosage slowly. This continues until a helpful, therapeutic dosage is reached. If a therapeutic dosage is not found, and it appears that the teen is being overmedicated (he appears tired and lethargic) then the psychia-trist will switch to Medication B and begin the process all over again. It may take several weeks to find the right dosage of the right medication.

Although this trial and error process can be tedious and frustrating, it is somewhat minimized or offset by the fact that these types of medica-tions go in and out of the bloodstream extremely quickly. Ritalin may stay active in the system for only a few hours. Thus, it is possible to change dosages and change medications relatively quickly, without a lengthy time lag from trial to trial. This same characteristic also helps to mitigate the dangers of any potential side effects. Thus, if a teenager does experience a negative side effect, it should subside relatively quickly. For example, he takes Ritalin in the morning before school and it gives him a headache. If he comes home and goes to bed, the medication in the bloodstream, and the headache, should be gone by early evening.

SIDE EFFECTS AND MEDICATION "HOLIDAYS"

Many things have been written and reported about various side effects for these types of stimulant medications, especially Ritalin. One potential side effect that has received particular attention is a decrease in appetite and resulting weight loss. Although this is true, to a degree, this is not as severe as some people believe or as has been reported in the media. Ritalin and some other stimulants do cause a decrease in appetite, resulting in weight loss or a decrease in the rate of weight gain. The evidence suggests that this phenomenon corrects itself within about one year, however. That is, after the initial loss of appetite and the decrease in rate of growth, teens acclimate to the medication and catch up to where they would have been if they had never taken the medication in the first place. Thus, it appears that this side effect is short lived and has no long-term consequences.*

Despite this rebound effect, the side effect of weight loss can be worrisome for someone who naturally tends to be thin, or for an athlete who is concerned about his physical size and development. Others may be concerned because this rebound effect may take longer than twelve months. Remember, different people react to these medications differently, and different bodies metabolize them and acclimate to them at their own rates.

One way to combat this weight loss is to not take the medication every day, but to schedule in what is sometimes called a medication holiday. For example, some parents have been able to limit teenagers' weight loss by not giving them their medication on the weekends. The teenager simply eats them out of house and home on the weekends (which is not all that unusual), and this offsets any weight loss during the week. In this same vein, some parents have decided to not administer the teenager's meds over the summer or during vacations. This too helps to offset any weight loss, and serves to give the teenager a break. On the surface, this sounds like a fine idea. After all, most of the time, the teen has been prescribed his medication because of difficulties in school, so if he is not in school, he probably doesn't need the medication, right? For some teenagers, this is true, and it makes perfect sense to give them a medication holiday. Some, however, *like* how they feel

---

* It may be more accurate to say that no long-term consequences have been rigorously and reliably demonstrated through research. There are no studies examining how these medications affect an individual after taking them for 20 years. Those studies simply have not been conducted because people have not been taking these medications for ADHD for that long.

when they are on their meds. They feel more focused and more in control of themselves. They feel calmer and more confident when they play sports or interact with friends. (Often, this is more important to teenagers than how they are doing in school.) Don't assume that you are doing your teen a favor by giving him a period of time off the meds. Talk with your teen and have him be part of the decision.

Another option besides stimulants is a new medication, Stratera, which was specifically designed as an alternative to stimulants. Stratera has its own set of issues, however. Because Stratera has only recently begun to be used to treat ADHD, less information is available about it. It does have some advantages over the stimulants, however. It appears to be easier to determine the correct, therapeutic dosage than it is with stimulants. Also, taking several doses of a stimulant in the same day can sometimes make a person feel like they are on a seesaw, always going up and down. Because Stratera stays in the bloodstream longer, the effects are much more even and consistent. Finally, Stratera is not associated with a loss of appetite the way Ritalin and other stimulants are. Thus, if appetite loss is a side effect that is causing a significant amount of worry or concern for you or your teen, then Stratera may be a better option. As is the case with all of these medications, only your physician can prescribe them. If you have questions, speak with your physician about your concerns.

MEDS AND MANAGEMENT

In many ways, the best analogy for treating ADHD is diabetes. Diabetes is still serious, but it used to be a horrific, debilitating, potentially deadly disease. We often overlook this today, because now it can usually be 100% controlled by learning how to test one's own blood and consistently taking insulin or other medications. Those suffering from diabetes can lead full, happy, and active lives. The medications do not cure diabetes, but they do help those with the disease manage it. The same is true for ADHD and the medications we use to treat it.

Therapy

In addition to medication, therapy is often very useful for teenagers with ADHD. Even though the research shows that by far, the most effective way to help a teenager concentrate and focus their attention better is medication, therapy can often help a teen develop coping skills, improve self-esteem and other secondary issues. Chapter 14 offers some suggestions on helping a resistant teen consider therapy, including alternatives such as family or group therapies.

All therapies, no matter what the diagnosis of the teenager, will be somewhat unique and geared towards the individual. Almost any form of therapy one chooses for a teenager with ADHD will have certain similarities, however. First of all, teenagers should be treated like teenagers and not like children. Treatment should be very open about the fact that the teen has been diagnosed with having ADHD, and it should include some education about what ADHD is and what it is not. If we expect teenagers to take responsibility for themselves and to be a part of the solution, at the very least they need be able to understand why they have certain tendencies and why they exhibit certain behaviors. Teens need to know that these tendencies do not make them bad, but that they need to take ownership of making improvements in the future. Treatment helps them identify their strengths and weaknesses and develop coping strategies. This may include helping them develop organizational skills, such as teaching them how to make a schedule for daily routines (getting up and going to school, doing homework, etc.), create daily "to do lists," and developing mechanisms for writing down, completing, and turning in homework. Therapy will also focus on helping them to identify their feelings and frustrations and to learn to express these feelings verbally in a way that will help to solve the situation rather than to make it worse. They will learn to see how their actions and attitudes affect those around them. Finally, most treatments for teenagers with ADHD will include some work on anger management and developing strategies to help tolerate frustration.

Tips for Parents

In addition to helping the teenager enter therapy, there are several things that parents can do to help. Before we discuss this, however, please note once again that just because the parent steps in and tries to help correct something that is a difficulty in a teenager's life, that does not in any way mean that the parent has caused this difficulty. And just because the parent did not cause the problem does not mean that they cannot help fix it.

Proactive, not Reactive

First of all, despite the tension, anger, and anxiety that having a teenager with ADHD can cause in a family, parents must maintain the desired hierarchy in the family. This means that parents set the guidelines and parameters in the family. And most importantly, this means that parents should never find themselves in a position of being reactive to their teenager. Whatever the situation, whether it's ADHD, depression, or simply an angry young man, parents need to calm themselves down first, then try to calm the teenager down, and only then should they try to resolve the problem. Parents should never feel as though they are reacting to a situation or a demand created by their son or daughter. They need to change the situation so that they are being proactive and are addressing the situation in a way that they think is best. This, and not punishment, is the most important and most powerful aspect of sending a teen to his room (or for a younger child, putting him in time out).

One vital component of being able to do this is to ensure that both parents are on the same page in terms of their philosophies on parenting and their expectations for their child and for each other. This allows the parents to provide reinforcement, positive feedback, and, when appropriate, constructive criticism to each other. In single-parent homes, it is imperative that the parent develop a support system to provide this feedback and encouragement.

Structure, Positive Reinforcement, and Organization

The very nature of ADHD almost ensures that parents of teenagers with this disorder spend a significant amount of time structuring and disciplining their adolescent. Although different strategies will be more or less helpful for different families, some general guidelines may be helpful. Punishment is a very useful tool, but it should not be a parent's only tool. While it has its place, it's generally, more effective the less it is used. Many teens with ADHD have received (in fact, have elicited) a great deal of negative feedback. Playing into this pattern only serves to reinforce whatever anger and insecurity may be fueling their behavior. In addition to punishment, parents also need to rely on rewards, positive reinforcement, and praise to help structure their teens' behaviors. Positive reinforcement, which tells the teen what to do, is generally more effective than punishment, which tells the teen what *not* to do—and it will bolster a teen's self-esteem and help to decrease his frustration.

Teenagers who have difficulty focusing their attention or persisting with long, boring tasks sometimes have difficulty delaying gratification and waiting for rewards, reinforcement, and positive feedback. In such cases, even very tempting rewards, which seemed enticing at the beginning of a task, lose their power to motivate as the task wears on. If this happens, several small, more immediate reinforcers interspersed throughout the task will be more effective and easier to provide than one large reinforcer at the end. For additional information, see Chapter 7.

In addition to these options for responding to a teenager's behavior, it is helpful to teach and promote the skills that will help prevent negative behaviors in the first place. For a teenager with ADHD, this often means providing them with structure, structure, and more structure. Although they may rebel against this, it is often, in hindsight, what they describe as craving the most.

Jack, a 17-year-old high-school student, had been diagnosed as having ADHD when he was in fourth grade and had had moderate to severe difficulties in school throughout his academic career. Although very intelligent, Jack just never applied himself to his schoolwork. Something would always get in the way and distract him. When he was able to sit down and try to work, it felt overwhelming and he would just stare at the computer screen. Whenever his parents would try to help him, whether by coaching or threatening punishment, he would become angry, belligerent, and disrespectful. His parents, not wanting to make matters worse, would back off and never follow through with their threats. Finally, during Jack's junior year in high school, Jack's parents were able to set some very clear, concrete guidelines for Jack to follow. He was to start his homework every day at the same specified time. It was always to be done in the dining room and to be checked by his mother or father. He was required to work for ten minutes before taking a short break (to get something to eat, go online, etc.). Jack's grades improved immediately. By the end of the marking period, he had a B average and was permitted to get his driver's license as a reward. Moving forward, however, Jack's parents did not feel that they could continue to enforce their homework rules now that the incentive of the driver's license was no longer available. Jack said that he liked doing well in school and would try to make himself stick to the rules, but he was unable to do so. With some prodding, Jack's parents reinstated the rules and enforced them. Even though there was nothing being held over his head, Jack complied with only minimal opposition. After a second marking period of good grades, Jack was able to admit that he appreciated having this structure and that it was a relief having someone else be in charge so that he didn't have to discipline himself. In time, as he continued to see results, Jack accepted the benefits of maintaining this type of schedule. When he applied to colleges, he specifically looked for schools with programs that would help him with structure and self-discipline. Consistent structure, and the ability to safely test the limits of this structure, allows the teenager to develop a sense of security, and also to learn how to create structure for himself.

It may be helpful to overtly teach your teenager organizational skills and how to create structure for himself. This may include reminding him to make a list or agenda of what he needs to accomplish for a certain project or within a certain period of time. Help him break this list down into manageable steps. Allow frequent short breaks or other frequent, small rewards for positive reinforcement. Help them to set reasonable time limits for each step and reasonable expectations and contingency plans for any missteps that may occur.

Process, not Just Content

Finally, as we mentioned above, individuals with ADHD tend to be impulsive. They express their feelings, frustrations, and desires without thinking. For teenagers, this often comes out as angry, disrespectful words and behaviors. In addition to talking with your teenager about *what* he said or did (there is always a place for this), you'll also need to address *how* he did it—in other words, address the process as well as the content.

Beyond discussing the fact that your teen's room is a disaster (and whether or not you have the right to ask him to pick it up) but also the fact that he is being disrespectful—not looking at you, rolling his eyes, interrupting, and so on—while talking about this with you.

Designate a Case Manager

As parents try to help their teenagers cope with ADHD, it can feel over-whelming for both parties. For parents, this can be compounded by having to communicate with a myriad of professionals—teachers, the principal, the psychologist, the pediatrician, and the tutor—all of whom insist that their perspective is the most important. It is sometimes worth-while to take the time to coordinate all the pieces of treatment (letting the left hand know what the right hand is doing, and making sure that the left foot and the right foot are going in the same direction). Other-wise, it all tends to run together into one big confusing (and ineffec-tive) morass. If at all possible, try to designate one of the professionals as the case manager, responsible for coordinating with all the others. If this is not possible, it is wise to take on this role yourself. Despite how time-consuming this may seem, it will likely save you time, effort, and frustration in the long run.

Parents often ask us, "How long will my son have to take medica-tion?" "Will my daughter outgrow this?" "When will my kid be cured?" Think of the baseball player Nolan Ryan. He is a Hall of Fame pitcher and arguably one of the greatest baseball players of all time. When he first came up to the Major Leagues, Nolan Ryan had difficulty control-ling the location of his pitches, a problem with which he struggled throughout his career. He never fully corrected or cured this tendency, but he was able to learn to cope with it and, as a result, was able to go on to have an incredibly successful career. His difficulty controlling his location was not a handicap or an impediment to his career, just a ten-dency. With a lot of hard work, extra practice, and the determined mindset that although these control problems would recur from time to time, he would be able to work through these difficulties, Ryan be-came one of the best ever in his chosen field. The same is true for a teenager with ADHD. People with ADHD have certain tendencies that may include difficulty concentrating, being impulsive, having difficulty organizing themselves, and so on. In all likelihood, they will probably continue to have these same tendencies, to a greater or lesser degree, throughout their lives. But these tendencies do not have to be overwhelming and do not necessarily need to become impediments or handicaps. With work, motivation, and the development of certain skills, resources (such as medication), and coping strategies, teens with ADHD can thrive.

CHAPTER 12

SIZE TWO AND I AM STILL FAT!

Eating Disorders

What Are Eating Disorders?

Eating disorders, which include anorexia and bulimia, are among the most serious psychological disorders our teenagers face today. These potentially life-threatening disorders are also incredibly difficult and painful for the parents of teenagers. This chapter will examine what eating disorders are, what help parents can offer, and the treatment options available for both teenagers and their families.

According to the American Psychiatric Association, about 0.5% to 1% of adolescents and young adults have anorexia. Although both males and females may suffer from anorexia, the overwhelming majority— about 90%—of anorexics are female (American Psychiatric Association, 1994). Symptoms for anorexia include a refusal to maintain body weight, which results in the individual weighing not more than 85% of what is expected for their age and height. In addition, people with anorexia have an intense, though irrational fear, of being overweight. This fear is so powerful that individuals with anorexia actually have a drastically skewed body image: although everyone else will tell them they are thin, even frighteningly so, these individuals actually see themselves as being fat or overweight. Another term for this is *body dysmorphia* or *body dysmorphic disorder*. For women to receive a full diagnosis of anorexia, they must have missed at least three consecutive menstrual cycles. Finally, between 5% and 20% of anorexics die as a result of cardiac abnormalities brought on by the disease. Anorexics who have had the condition longer are at greater risk (Zerbe, 1995).

Bulimia, somewhat more prevalent, is found in approximately 1% to 3% of adolescents, and like anorexia, is significantly more common in women than in men. Approximately 90% of individuals with bulimia are women (American Psychiatric Association, 1994). According to the strict diagnostic criteria, bulimics habitually binge by consuming a large amount of food in a short period of time, and have a sense of a lack of control over their eating during this episode. They then partake in recurrent inappropriate behavior to compensate for these binges, including self-induced vomiting, misusing laxatives or diuretics, and over-exercising. In addition, people who suffer from bulimia often report that their sense of self-worth is unduly influenced by their weight and their body shape. A full diagnosis of bulimia requires that this cycle of bingeing and purging must have occurred at least twice a week for a minimum of three months.

In addition to these specific diagnostic criteria for anorexia and bulimia, researchers have found several associated phenomena. Thirty-five percent of normal dieters progress onto what is considered "pathological dieting," and of these pathological dieters, 20% to 25% progress onto a partial eating disorder. Of this group, approximately 30% to 45% develop either full anorexia or full bulimia (Shisslak, 1995). According to the Office on Women's Health, a 1997 study of students nationwide found that more than 4% had taken laxatives or diet pills, or had vomited, for weight control purposes. One of the most frightening findings may be that 70% of sixth grade girls report that they first became concerned about their weight between the ages of 9 and 11 (National Women's Health Information Center, 2000).

Who Develops Anorexia or Bulimia?

One of the biggest misconceptions about both of these eating disorders is that they are simply disorders of behavior—that by controlling the behavior, it is possible to effectively treat or even cure the disorder. You might find yourself saying or thinking, "Just eat. If you just eat, everything will be fine. You should be able to just eat." The problem is that eating disorders are not isolated to behaviors, but also involve disordered thoughts and feelings. Individuals with eating disorders have a poorly developed sense of control, either of themselves or of their surroundings. They also have a compromised ability to cope with anxiety, and they often have a poorly defined and developed sense of who they are and how they fit into their world. Individuals with eating disorders may also have a skewed view of how healthy relationships should work, how they fit into a relationship, and how they should interact with others.

Researchers have identified certain factors that might predispose an individual to develop anorexia or bulimia. These factors include being in a middle or upper socioeconomic group, or working or aspiring to work in a profession that strongly emphasizes thinness or appearance, such as modeling or acting. A history of obesity that once resulted in stringent dieting behaviors can also be a risk factor for developing anorexia or bulimia, as does a history of sexual abuse, physical abuse, or some other psychological trauma. Having a close relative with a history of an eating disorder can also place an individual at risk. Certain personality characteristics may predispose someone towards anorexia or bulimia, including low self-esteem coupled with very high expectations, and difficulty identifying and verbalizing emotions. This is particularly true in regards to anger and negative feelings. Women who develop anorexia tend to be overly cautious. They're fearful of change, very orderly, and somewhat perfectionistic. Those who develop bulimia tend to be somewhat disorganized and impulsive, which also places them somewhat at risk for suicide or other self-injurious behavior, even if it is not specifically associated with the eating disorder.

Families and Eating Disorders

Much has been made about eating disorders and the role that families and parents play in their development. The vast majority of professionals now agree that parents do not cause eating disorders. Some dynamics of the family may contribute to the development of an eating disorder, or may even enable an eating disorder, but this is a far cry from actually causing an eating disorder. Nevertheless, many parents feel intensely guilty when their child is diagnosed with an eating disorder. As is the case with other disorders such as ADHD, depression, or any other type of anxiety or conflict during the teenage years, even if the parents don't cause it, they still have some of the responsibility to help fix it. They can be very powerful agents of change in their teenagers' lives.

Let us look at some of the ways that families and family communication patterns play into and support an eating disorder. Most, if not all, families have rules. Some of these rules are very obvious and overt, such as, "You need to clean up after yourself," or, "It's Johnny's job to take the garbage out, and it's Lisa's job to help do the dishes." Other rules are much more subtle, and often the people in the family don't even realize that these rules exist. Examples of these rules would be, "It's not okay to get angry. We shouldn't fight even if we disagree with each other." Families with anorexic or bulimic children often have very inconsistent rules. One consistent rule in the families of children with eating disorders, however, is that it is neither safe nor acceptable to express feelings openly. Negative feelings, such as anger, are considered dangerous or in poor taste, and they are expected to be avoided, ignored, and kept inside. Another typical characteristic in families where one or more teens has an eating disorder is either a skewed or an inconsistent sense of control. Children and teenagers in these families typically report that their parents are either too controlling or are too uninvolved. Sometimes teenagers in these families report that their parents vacillate between one extreme and the other. In any case, either being overcontrolling or undercontrolling is not experienced by the children as being supportive, or as fostering their own sense of control and autonomy, and their own confidence in asserting themselves. Neither extreme fosters a healthy sense of independence, but instead promotes a sense of dependence or an unhealthy aversion to feelings of dependence.

Further, these families tend to be somewhat rigid in terms of the roles that different people in the family occupy. It is very difficult for these families to adapt and change as the individuals in these families themselves grow and adapt and change over time. For example, one member in a family may have the role of being the child or the youngest, the one that everyone else needs to nurture. As this individual grows and matures and wants to assert her independence, such a family might have difficulty allowing this child to act in a more adult manner, and in some ways, serves to keep her in that role of being dependent. The families of children with eating disorders also tend to place a strong emphasis on physical appearance. Just like the individuals themselves, these families tend to value a person's physical appearance and attractiveness with to associate this self-worth.

Another aspect of these families is that they tend to have poor or inconsistent boundaries. What we mean by poor boundaries is not simply that people in the family do not get enough privacy. This is only part of it. In addition, people's roles and responsibilities in the family often get blurred or confused. An example of this would be when a teenager needs to take on the responsibility of making decisions or performing other tasks that would be better handled by the adults in the family. Another example of poor boundaries is when the feelings or anxieties of one individual overflow and end up affecting other family members. A teenager is anxious about exams, for example, and so the entire family, parents and siblings, become anxious as well. It's one thing to be empathetic to another's feelings, but when all is said and done, it is still the individual's problem, the individual's emotion, and ultimately, the individual's responsibility to address these concerns. There's a difference between being supportive of someone else's plight and taking on those feelings and frustrations yourself. Now in Chapter 3, we mentioned that teenagers often make parents feel the way the teens are feeling. This is called projective identification, and it is, explicitly, a blurring of boundaries. Remember, however, when a teenager is making you feel they way they are feeling, the goal is to free yourself up from this dynamic and to *not* be so reactive to their feelings. Projective identification is useful as a tool because it gives us insight into what the teen is feeling, not because we want to continue that pattern. In this way, projective identification is analogous to a medical symptom, such as pain in the abdomen. If you have pain in a certain location, it gives the physician useful information or clues as to what is going on, but we still want to stop the pain.

Talking With Your Teen About an Eating Disorder

The first step in helping your child deal with an eating disorder is to talk with her about it. This topic should be discussed the same way any important, frightening, and even potentially overwhelming issue should be discussed with your teen. Take some time and plan out exactly what you want to say and how you want to say it. First, define your goals. This will help you to decide what you're going to talk about, and how you want to address this. Your primary goal for this talk is to express your concerns—after all, you wouldn't be having this talk if you hadn't noticed that something was amiss and become concerned. The next major goal is to emotionally communicate to your teenager that you love her, you're there to support her, and that these issues, are not insurmountable. Finally, your last goal will be to discuss some type of treatment plan or intervention, or even just to acknowledge the idea that treatment or some type of intervention might be needed, regardless of what this is. We will talk more about specific treatment options and what these entail below.

Notice that the goal at this point should not be to control your teen's eating patterns. If this *is* your goal, this conversation will probably be very frustrating for all parties involved, and will likely be doomed to failure. At this point, you just want to be able to raise the topic, discuss things openly, and have everyone to express their feelings, concerns, and fears.

Pick a time when everybody is calm, and bring up the topic on your own terms. This will be better than waiting for something to happen that makes you bring up the topic as a reaction, rather than on a more proactive basis. Make sure that you set aside enough time to go through everything you need to say, and that you have your ideas and your major points organized in your mind. Sometimes, you may find it easier to write down notes for yourself. When organizing your thoughts, again remember that the emotions that you communicate are as important as the content and the ideas of what you say. As we have stressed in other situations, not only do you want to express what you're feeling, but you also want to model for your teenager how to discuss topics that may be unpleasant, awkward, or even painful.

Have realistic expectations for this talk, and realize that at this stage, resistance is inevitable. More than likely, you can expect her to become somewhat defensive and to try to deny or explain away some of your concerns. If so, you don't necessarily need to stop her from going through this. This is the beginning of communication. Take the time to listen—your teen may have some valid points—but you don't necessarily have to agree. Even if this discussion does not, at least initially, result in getting your teenager into treatment, it can still be very useful if its only benefit is opening up the lines of communication about eating disorders between you and your teenager.

Treatment

Eating disorders generally require professional intervention. Research shows that teenagers are significantly more likely to fully recover from an eating disorder when intervention takes place early in the course of the disorder. The parents' and the family's job is to get the individual into treatment, and to be supportive of the treatment, not to actually try to cure the eating disorder. It works better to leave that part to the professionals. Nevertheless, it can be very difficult to get a teenager into treatment for an eating disorder.

One option or one technique for this is what Abigail Natenshon defines as an intervention. An intervention is "a meeting of caring, loving others who come together to make a collective appeal to the eating-disordered individual for her recovery." (Natenshon, p. 233). After the parents have identified an eating disorder as a problem, an intervention involves confronting the eating-disordered individual as a group, and using whatever means necessary and whatever resources are available, to convince this person to go into treatment. It is much more effective to do this as a group rather than one-on-one. This shows your teenager that her entire family, the people who care about her, feel this is best for her. An intervention like this also underscores the hierarchy in the family. This is not simply a discussion of what is happening-that was the previous step or stage. This is a decision by the parents that will be backed up and enforced by the family as a whole.

The most effective treatment for eating disorders is a multimodal approach. This means that several professionals from different, varied disciplines are a part of one person's treatment team. These multi-disciplinary teams typically include any or all of the following: a psychiatrist to treat the patient with medication; an internist or other medical doctor to treat other related medical concerns that may arise; an individual therapist, usually a psychologist or a social worker; a family therapist, usually a different psychologist or social worker; a nutritionist; and the parents.

The parents are vital members of the treatment team. It is their role to advocate for their teenager and to get them the services that they need. Perhaps most importantly, parents often assume the role of case manager. With so many professionals involved, it can be difficult to coordinate services, to coordinate doctor's visits and to make sure that one treatment team member is aware of what the other treatment team members are doing. Effective organization and coordination of the treatment team is often what makes the difference between an effective and an ineffective treatment, and parents should be prepared take on this role. Parents in the same family forget to convey information all the time (Everyone has had a conversation along the lines of, "What do you mean she has a game tonight? I thought that was next week.") Expect the professionals working with your daughter to make some of the same mistakes.

One of the first tasks of the treatment team (or sometimes the first professional that you contact) is to evaluate the situation and decide how best to administer treatment. Depending on the severity of the eating disorder, many different options exist for treatment. In acute cases, where the teen's eating disorder is so severe that she is in danger of doing permanent harm to herself, it might make sense to at least begin treatment as an inpatient in a hospital. In less severe cases, treatment can be administered on an outpatient basis in which the patient sees the different treatment team members once or twice a week or maybe even just once or twice a month. In some areas, options for day hospital treatment exist. In this model, patients go home every night, but every day they return to the hospital for more intensive treatment than what is typically administered on an outpatient basis. Finally, in cases where the eating disorder is long-standing and more resistant to treatment, it makes sense to treat the individual in a residential setting.

One commonly held myth about eating disorders is that individuals with eating disorders never fully recover, that they're always in the process of recovery, such as addicts or alcoholics. This is not true. With early intervention, individuals can completely and fully recover from both anorexia and bulimia. Be aware, however, that progress during treatment for an eating disorder can be very uneven. Backsliding and regression are typical and are an expected part of the recovery process. Knowing this doesn't always make it less frustrating, however. Remember, in addition to simply being a set of behaviors, an eating disorder is a means of coping for the teenager. Treatment very specifically seeks to remove this coping strategy, which usually leads the patient to become extremely anxious and blatantly resist the treatment.

One type of resistance to treatment is splitting team members. At different times during the treatment, the teenager may align herself with different team members and against other team members. She may tend to view certain team members as "good," "helpful," or "nice," and others "bad," "mean," or "insensitive." Problems arise when the teen is able to seduce others (friends, family, or other treatment team members) into playing into her point of view. Part of the team's function—and part of the parent's role as a case manager—is to help maintain the cohesion and the communication of the treatment team, without allowing the patient to split and fragment it.

Another important part of the recovery process is for parents to identify, acknowledge, and work through some of their own frustrations and discouragements. This is true not just for the expected regressions and backsliding in the recovery process, but for the eating disorder in general. Remember, although parents do not cause an eating disorder, sometimes their fears, frustrations, reactions, and expectations play into it, and may enable some of the behaviors. By openly addressing and acknowledging your own fears and frustrations, you can model for your daughter exactly what you would like her to do through treatment.

Treatment should not be viewed as an event, but rather as a long, multistep process. In many cases, after the initial intensive treatment, it is probably unrealistic to expect that progress will continue or even be maintained without some type of follow-up and aftercare plan. This may include halfway houses specifically designed for individuals recovering from eating disorders, support groups, and finally, continued outpatient treatment with either a psychologist, a psychiatrist, or a social worker. In any of these cases, it is very important for the parents to continue to look at themselves and to maintain their role as part of the treatment team.

During the treatment process, remember that weight gain alone is not equivalent to recovery for an eating disorder. Again, an eating disorder is not simply about a set of eating behaviors. It's the thoughts, feelings, coping mechanisms, and self-evaluation that go along with it. Comprehensive treatment for an eating disorder does not just focus on eating behaviors, or on the feelings driving these behaviors. Rather, effective treatment needs to focus on both, and progress can be measured in many different ways. Placing too much focus on one and not enough on the other can reduce the treatment's effectiveness.

What More Can Parents Do?

In addition to getting your teen into treatment for an eating disorder, what can parents do? First and foremost, as is the case with other disorders and with just having an adolescent child in general, parents need to take care of themselves: take time on their own, talk with friends and family members, and if necessary, join support groups or go into therapy themselves to get the support that they need. The second thing the parents need to do is to identify and accept their own limitations. This means accepting that it is neither your responsibility, nor is it within your power, to try to control your child's eating. Rather than trying to control her, you need to help your teenager take responsibility for herself and see herself as an effective, flexible, and independent individual. In this way, you are helping her develop healthy boundaries. For example, while recovering, do not let the teenager control the food in the house for the rest of the family. Don't let her turn normal, healthy family activities (sitting down at the table for dinner, doing chores, or cleaning up) into fights or arguments about food. Rather than allowing her to put you in a position where you end up taking responsibility for controlling the food, help her do this for herself. Do not participate in cover-ups about eating, binges, or purging. When your daughter does binge, she needs take responsibility for replacing the food.

Lastly, parents must model and help facilitate the development of positive, healthy communication patterns. Strive to make communication open, flexible, and not too focused on food or eating. We suggest that parents deemphasize weight and appearance, and not give their advice or opinions about these topics. Help your teen focus more on how she feels than on how she looks.

The following is a list of concrete dos and don'ts for parents to help their teenagers cope with eating disorders.

- Help your teenager develop high self-esteem and self-acceptance.

- Help her to trust internal food regulation—to eat when she is hungry and to stop when she is satiated, not when she feels she looks thin or fat or when she can fit into a certain outfit.

- Try to minimize external food cues. If she tends to binge, reduce temptation by not leaving food out.

- Avoid forced hunger or deprivation, such as putting her on a diet.

- Try to maximize satisfaction with the eating experience. Avoid having emotional conversations while eating, and try to minimize struggles over food.

- Allow children and teenagers appropriate, but not unlimited, food responsibilities such as including helping to shop for, plan, and prepare meals.

- Educate your teen about good nutrition.

- Try to involve the entire family in appropriate physical activities.

- And finally, become a role model yourself for all of these rules.

Healthy Relationships

As we've said earlier in this chapter, eating disorders are not simply disorders in behavior. They are also disorders in how your teenager interacts and relates to others. One way to promote recovery, and to maintain recovery, is by helping your teenager develop and maintain healthier, more adaptive, and flexible relationships, both with others and with herself. One of the keys to this is communication. Help your teenager develop healthy, open, and flexible communication patterns. Rather than restricting what she feels, help her identify and express all her emotions, especially the negative ones. Helping your teenager to learn to express her feelings in an appropriate and effective verbal manner decreases the need for her to have to cope with these feelings in other, less adaptive ways.

Foster your teen's self-respect based on all of who she is and her abilities, not simply on her appearance. Help her see that she is worthwhile regardless of how much she weighs or how she looks.

Help her achieve healthy boundaries, including developing a healthy sense of privacy, a sense of personal responsibility, and an ability to identify and accept her own feelings as opposed to those of others'. Help her to develop a sense of independence and effectiveness. This requires a balance between being supportive and nurturing, and imposing structure. The goal is to develop a more authoritative relationship with your teenager, as opposed to an authoritarian relationship. (See Chapter 4).

Finally, aside from how your teenager is coping with her eating disorder, help her see the positives in herself. Make a point of highlighting her other good qualities aside from her weight and appearance, and show her the positive roles she fills in the family and in her relationships with others. Reinforce her successes, especially in terms of her interactions and relationships with others. As her self-esteem and self-confidence improves, there will be less of a need for her to resort to rigid, disordered eating patterns as a method for coping.

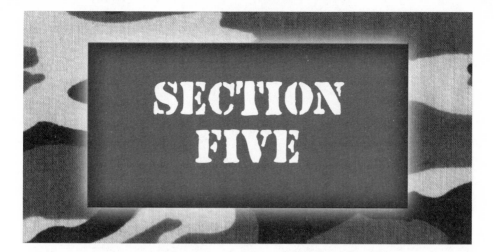

SECTION FIVE

Sustaining Survival for the Long Term

CHAPTER 13

SOMEBODY TO LEAN ON

Resources for Healthy Development and Help for the Hard Times

Our teenagers need a great deal from us: support, love, understanding, structure, and help developing a positive view of themselves and healthy social interaction skills. Parents can't always do it all on their own. Sometimes, it is not only helpful but necessary and responsible to look for other supports. What resources do parents have to help them help their teenagers navigate this very difficult and trying time in their lives?

Your Pediatrician

Your pediatrician is probably your first, best phone call. Pediatricians have experience working with hundreds of kids and teenagers, and more than likely, they've heard your concern before with other patients. Even for questions that are not necessarily medical in nature, such as concerns about your teen's maturity or social/emotional development, this is often a good place to start. They know a lot of the resources in the area and they are usually familiar with what other parents and teenagers in your position are doing. In addition, people in your community with programs or activities to offer you or your teenager know that all parents and teenagers have some kind of doctor. As a rule, they advertise and market to pediatricians. The net result is that most pediatricians have a drawer full of information about activities and resources for both parents and teenagers that they're just waiting to share with you. These resources often include community activities, other professionals in the area such as social workers, psychologists, psychiatrists, or even chiropractors who might be useful to you; or programs for teenagers with special needs.

Your Teenager's School

The second major general resource you have is your teenager's school. Your best contact person at the school will probably be the guidance counselor. As with pediatricians, anyone and everyone in the community with programs, activities, or expertise to offer to teenagers contacts guidance counselors. Guidance counselors work with hundreds of teenagers, and they know what teenagers are involved in, what's been helpful, and what hasn't been helpful. In addition, guidance counselors have regular, frequent contact with your teenager's teachers, and these teachers let the guidance counselors know if there are any concerns and what, if anything, your son or daughter needs. Guidance counselors can also help you find out which activities and resources available to your child through the school. This can include access to professionals such as school psychologists, social workers, or speech and language therapists, or lists of school clubs and organizations available to your child.

Tapping into Extracurricular Activities

What do Teens Gain From Activities?

As a rule, we prefer that teenagers are involved in at least one ongoing major extracurricular activity at all times. This can include sports, musical activities such as chorus or band, or performing arts such as dance or drama, playing a musical instrument, or becoming involved in a club or other organization at school. We like to see teens involved in these types of things for several reasons. Of course, they learn the activity around which the club or the team is organized. You learn journalism on the school newspaper, you learn how to act or sing or dance if you are involved with the school musical, and so on. For our purposes, however, this is the least important reason. Teenagers should certainly enjoy whatever activity they take up, but the content of the activity is not the most important thing that they get from it. Rather, teenagers learn how to interact with each other in a structured or a semi-structured environment: they learn social skills, how to feel comfortable and confident in social situations, how to assert themselves, how to give and take, and how to compromise. And finally, lest we forget, they learn how to have fun.

In addition to learning how to interact with others, teenagers learn a great deal about themselves through these activities. Hopefully, as they see that they have skills and abilities that other people value, these activities will help them to view themselves as effective, confident, worthwhile individuals. These activities also help them to identify and define who they are. As far back as the 1950s, psychologists have looked at the teenage years as a time when people begin to explore, formulate, and crystallize their identities. There's a great deal of experimentation at this time as teenagers try out different personas to see what feels right. To a large extent, many of us define ourselves by what we do. This is especially true for teenagers. Ask a teenager who they are and they'll say, "I'm a baseball player. I'm a guitar player. I'm a writer. I'm an artist." They define themselves by what they do and the activities in which they succeed. Sports, clubs, music, and other activities help teenagers to formulate a cohesive, crystallized sense of who they are. If they are successful at these activities, then hopefully they will develop a sense of themselves as being positive and confident. Group activities, where teens can interact with each other are especially helpful. Solitary activities or private lessons are also helpful, but don't provide the same types of social and interpersonal benefits.

As we know, teenagers use a lot of trial and error at this stage in their lives, and it is good and healthy for them to try out different activities. It is okay for teenagers to switch from one activity to the other. This must be done appropriately and responsibly, however. For example, it's okay for a teenager to join a basketball team and then decide that she really doesn't like basketball, and that she doesn't want to continue playing basketball for the rest of her life. She's made a commitment to her team and her teammates, however, and she needs to finish out the season. In addition to everything else, these activities can teach responsibility and commitment.

But remember to be flexible and not to go too far in applying the "responsibility principle." We had one family in which a teenager who had been taking karate lessons for about a year decided that he no longer wanted to take karate. His parents told him that he had made a commitment, and they decided that he could quit once he earned his black belt. This poor kid spent an extra five years taking karate lessons after he had decided that he was no longer interested. Think of all the other things he could have tried out, all the fun he could have had, and all the different ways he could have grown and developed if he had been allowed to try other activities. Although these types of activities can be tools for teaching responsibility, remember that there are other goals here as well.

School-Based Activities and Others

These days, school-sponsored activities go far beyond group sports. They may include the school newspapers, the yearbook, language clubs such as French Club or Spanish Club, writing clubs, science clubs, math clubs, gaming clubs such as a chess club, or any other club or activity that your school might have. Talk with your child's guidance counselor; he or she should have a list.

In addition to activities through the school system, there are also a number of wonderful clubs and activities outside the school system. Let us briefly discuss a few.

Many teenagers enjoy learning one or more martial arts. Martial arts have all the benefits we mentioned above, plus a number of other specific benefits. First and foremost, martial arts are absolutely wonderful at helping people develop self-esteem. There's a certain amount of confidence that comes with knowing that you can kick seven feet in the air or break a board with your elbow. In addition, good karate schools with good instructors are more concerned with teaching things like discipline, self-restraint, and respect than they are interested in teaching students how to kick and break boards. As long as the school or the instructor stresses the philosophical component inherent in these activities, plus the responsibility, self-restraint, and the respect that goes along with it, it can be a wonderful and formative experience for any teenager.

Another phenomenon that's been growing in popularity over the past couple of years are role-playing or strategy games. Many of the stores that sell these games and the equipment for them often have impromptu tournaments and sometimes even structured leagues. This can be a great activity for teenagers who don't have any particular interest in more traditional clubs and activities run through the schools. It gives them an opportunity to interact with their peers, to feel confident and successful, and to have positive peer interactions. For many, it's a way to fit in without having to have a specific skill, like playing the clarinet or knowing how to hit a baseball.

Another set of organized activities run outside of the schools are church or religious youth groups. These provide all the positives of some of the other clubs and programs we've discussed—increasing self-esteem, learning to be comfortable and confident in social situations, and so on— but they have other benefits as well. Just like gaming clubs, teens don't need to have a special skill to be a part of a youth group. Furthermore, most youth groups specifically focus on providing a structure and a framework to help teenagers develop, mature, and explore their world. Some youth groups specifically focus on helping teenagers to interact with each other and to learn about themselves in the process.

Another added benefit of religious youth groups and religions in general is that they provide teenagers with rites of passage. Rites of passage signify growth, development, and acceptance by your peer group, and by the adult culture teens are trying to move into. These are exactly the issues and the topics that are important for teenagers. Unlike many societies, our society does not have many pre-made, accepted rites of passage. In many instances, rites of passage for teens in our society have devolved into one's first drink, one's first cigarette, one's first experiment with drugs, or one's first sexual experience. Youth groups can help replace these types of rites of passage with healthier, more adaptive rites that promote self-esteem, responsibility, independence, and the ability to be a part of a larger group.

Activities with Adult Interaction

In addition to these more peer-oriented activities, there are also activities that allow teenagers to develop a positive relationship with other caring and nurturing adults. These include Big Brother/Big Sister programs, apprenticeships, and mentor programs. Just like the peer programs already discussed, these types of programs help teenagers develop a sense of confidence, increase self-esteem, and foster a sense of independence.

BIG BROTHER/BIG SISTER

The most common and popular of these programs is Big Brother/Big Sister. In Big Brother or Big Sister, an older teenager or young adult is paired with a younger teenager or child with whom they spend one-on-one time doing recreational activities. This can be a good fit for someone who has lost a parent, or for someone whose family has gone through a divorce and is estranged from one parent. Having one-on-one time with a positive role model can be invaluable for many teenagers.

APPRENTICESHIPS

An apprenticeship program is a different way to spend quality one-on-one time with a positive adult role model. Technically, in an apprenticeship program, a teenager or young adult has already received some specialized training in a given trade or field. He or she then works under the close supervision of a master craftsman in that field, learning the finer points of the trade. So the content of what the adult and teenager do is very important in an apprenticeship. The teenager learns a trade that he or she will use throughout life. This by itself is invaluable. Like the Big Brother/Big Sister program, however, apprenticeships have other benefits: a teenager has the opportunity to spend one-on-one time with an adult who will be supportive and overtly invested in what the teen is doing. Again, this type of relationship can be extremely therapeutic for a teenager. The work-based structure of an apprenticeship program also helps teens to feel that the adult is spending time with them for a reason, not just out of pity or good intentions, which allows independent teens to save face.

MENTORSHIPS

Another way to get this type of quality one-on-one adult interaction is through a mentorship program. The idea of mentorship programs is quite new, and they are only found in certain parts of the country. In a mentorship program, an adult supervises a teenager or young adult one-on-one and almost acts as a life skills coach. Mentorship programs are intended for older teens or young adults who need help taking responsibility and becoming independent. It is a transitional step between living as a dependent child and moving out on your own and living independently. The adult checks up on the teen's living arrangement, on their schoolwork and their job performance, and works with them to manage the different responsibilities in their lives. They're adult authority figures who look over teens' shoulders, help them out, and provides support, structure, and guidance. Mentors do not do this as a hobby or charity, but as a full-time job. It is not a part-time activity but a full-time commitment. There's no official program to train them, and their backgrounds vary greatly from having almost no training to having a background in education or one of the other helping professions. The best way to find a mentor who has some experience and is good at what they do, is through a professional called an Educational Consultant. We will discuss what Educational Consultants are and the services that they provide later in this chapter.

Summer Programs

So far, all the programs and resources we've mentioned take place either year-round or during the academic year. Some programs are specific to the summer, however. Because they are "just over the summer," some people have the tendency to discount these resources, or to think of them as unhelpful or unimportant. To the contrary, some of these programs can be incredibly powerful, and can end up having a dramatic effect on a teenager's life.

CAMP

The most common summer programs are residential summer camps. There are many types of residential summer camps. Some are parts of large organizations that have hundreds of camps throughout the country, such as Boy Scout camps, Girl Scout camps, or YMCA camps. Others are smaller, independent camps. Some are specialty camps such as sports camps, arts camps, or foreign language camps. Some are more general, or classic camps.

The success of summer camp depends a great deal on the teen's (and his or her family's) goals. For example, your teenager may go to a camp looking for a specific activity or a specific group of activities, whether it's water-skiing and motor-boating, instruction in a particular sport, certain types of arts and crafts training, certain types of instruction in computers or other academic areas. Camps can be wonderful for this purpose.

As discussed with many of these programs, however, camps have other benefits far beyond those of the activities that they provide. Summer camps provide kids and teenagers with an excellent opportunity to fit in and to feel part of a group and to improve their peer relations. It allows them to feel confident in their interactions with others and in who they are. A good summer camp, where the focus is on the counseling, will make sure the kids and teenagers fit in well with their cabin mates or their tent mates, and that they feel a part of their cabin or their tent and the camp as a whole. This sense of belonging can be invaluable for teenagers, and is also exactly what most teenagers crave. Because residential camps immerse teenagers in their peer group 24 hours a day, the experiences one has at residential summer camps are often much more intense, and therefore much, much more helpful to teens than most of the clubs and activities through school. For this reason, there is a qualitative difference in the benefits a teenager can get from a residential camp versus a day camp. In fact, most day camps would not be appropriate for most teenagers. The best summer camps are not simply a collection of fun activities; they really feel like a family. One summer camp director we know describes a successful session at camp as having a majority of his campers, both boys and girls, breaking down and crying at the end of the session when they have to leave each other.

In addition, summer camps provide positive adult role models and a model for healthy peer interactions. Because it's 24 hours a day, there is no sidestepping issues that may arise with peers. Many teenagers are not exposed to this way of interacting with their friends in school. In addition, summer camps provide an opportunity to get away from some of the pressures of home and almost start new. Kids are who they are at camp, without having to deal with the reputations that they've already formed and the mistakes that they've already made. Good summer camps are places where they feel that they are not going to be judged. In many ways, summer camps can be very therapeutic. In terms of developing self-confidence and improved self-esteem, three or four weeks of a good summer camp program can be as helpful as several months of individual psychotherapy with a good psychologist.

For most kids, age 10 is usually a good time to start attending a summer camp. Many camps will accept campers up to age 15 or sometimes even older. In addition, camps provide options for older teenagers. Many camps have Counselor In Training (CIT) programs for teenagers 16 years old and older. This is not just *an* option but a *great* option for older teens. Working at a summer camp gives teens the exact same benefits that attending a summer camp as a camper provides. Many teens report that working at a summer camp can be more fun and more rewarding than being a camper at a summer camp. In addition to everything else, it teaches maturity, responsibility, and helps to develop a level of personal insight that's hard to match in any other setting. Working with kids or younger teenagers teaches anyone a lot about themselves. For a teenager who is angry at his or her parents and having difficulty following the rules, it can often be a very helpful intervention to be placed in an authority position for a couple of weeks—in effect, the teen has to learn to help be a parent to younger teenagers.

OUTWARD BOUND/NOLS

Teens can gain very powerful experiences through wilderness programs such as Outward Bound or National Outdoor Leadership School (NOLS). A summer at Outward Bound or NOLS can be a great experience for a teenager, but it tends to be more intense than working at a summer camp. In these programs, students (teenagers can earn high school and even college credits for these programs) participate in an intensive outdoor experience. This experience could be hiking and backpacking, rock climbing, canoeing, rafting, or even kayaking, sailing, or horseback riding. The students are outdoors, challenging themselves both physically and emotionally. Even more so than some of these residential summer camp programs, Outward Bound or a NOLS trip do an exceptional job of helping teenagers and young adults develop confidence and improve their self-esteem. An incredible sense of accomplishment, self-reliance, and independence comes from completing some of these trips.

In addition, most of these trips are designed so that participants will only be able to complete what they need to do by working with their peers as a unit. Trips focus on helping members develop cooperation skills and group dynamics are generally a central focus during the trip. These programs foster collaboration and leadership skills.

This is all in addition to the very real therapeutic value of being out in nature in a very beautiful area (trips occur in a variety of geographical locations), and being away from the home environment. Often, just this change in scenery can help teens and young adults change their perspective on themselves and their lives. At the end of these trips, participants generally report an increased sense of self-confidence, self-awareness, and maturity and a better sense of who they are and what their capabilities are.

Doctors and Therapists

The next set of resources for parents are doctors and therapists. Parents frequently ask us whether their son or daughter needs medication, therapy, or both. In a lot of ways, this is a very value-laden question. In some cases, it really matters what everyone involved feels more comfortable with. There is a growing body of evidence to show that both medication and psychotherapy, or "talk therapy," are quite effective in treating a wide range of clinical disorders, including depression.

What professionals should parents seek out to help teenagers with anxiety, depression, or any other types of stress or emotional difficulties? As we mentioned earlier, your pediatrician is often a good first step in finding a helping professional. Your pediatrician should be able you refer you to a variety of qualified helping professionals. Furthermore, most pediatricians feel comfortable prescribing stimulant medications for ADHD, or SSRIs (selective seratonin re-uptake inhibitors, a common type of drug that includes Prozac and Zoloft) for depression and anxiety. If these first straightforward options are not effective, then it might be a prudent to find a psychiatrist, a medical doctor trained in treating mental health issues and mood disorders with medication. Some psychiatrists are also trained to do some types of talk therapy as well. Again, the choice of medication versus therapy is often one of personal preference. Some disorders clearly respond better to one (medication for ADHD symptoms, for example) or the other (therapy for a phobia). But for many individuals, and for many issues, there is a choice. One way to conceptualize this is to think of medications as alleviating certain symptoms, while therapy focuses on more general coping strategies and ways of perceiving yourself and the world around you. And, in fact, we often find that a combination of the two works better than either one alone.

Choosing a Therapist

The general term for a professional who treats individuals by talking and listening, and through applying learning theory, is a therapist. Usually when we say therapist or psychotherapist, we're referring to a psychologist, a social worker, or a counselor. Technically, however, a therapist can be anyone with a high school diploma; anyone can call himself or herself a therapist. Therefore, when selecting a therapist, it is an extremely good idea to learn about each candidate's background, credentials, and training.

Psychologists, clinical social workers, and counselors are all licensed professionals. This means that they have a certain degree of training, they have demonstrated their proficiency in these techniques, they adhere to a professional code of ethics, and they are required to participate in significant continuing education. Although there's a great deal of overlap, there are differences between psychologists, social workers, and counselors. A psychologist is someone who has earned a doctoral-level degree in psychology, and who has become licensed in providing psychological services to the public. Psychologists are specifically trained in treating patients through psychotherapy by listening to them, talking to them, and applying different learning, cognitive, and personality theories to help intervene and promote change. In addition, most psychologists are specifically trained in research and are probably the best consumers of scientific psychological studies, and are best prepared to try to apply these research findings to their practice with patients. Another factor that separates psychologists from counselors and social workers is psychological testing. Although there are exceptions (some counselors and school psychologists), psychologists are the professionals who are specifically trained in administering, scoring, and interpreting psychological tests. These tests include personality assessments, cognitive or intellectual assessments, and other more specific tests such as those to provide or rule out specific diagnoses. They also administer an array of academic and vocational assessments.

Social workers, in contrast, are not doctoral-level professionals, but rather have earned a Master's degree in social work. They, too, are specifically trained in psychotherapy, working with patients by listening and talking with them. Where psychologists probably receive more training in terms of research and personality structure and theory, social workers receive more and better training in some of the social and societal factors that might affect individuals, and also in using different social services and resources in the community.

Counselors, who may include marriage counselors or marriage and family therapy counselors, are also Master's-level professionals trained in psychotherapy. In addition, some counselors have pursued extra training to allow them to administer certain types of tests and assessments under particular conditions.

So whom should your child or your family see for psychotherapy—a psychologist, a social worker, or a counselor? As with most things in this field, there's no one right straightforward answer to that question. Although we are psychologists, we refer and collaborate with many gifted therapists who are licensed social workers and counselors. In terms of choosing a therapist, it's probably most important to pick someone with whom both you and your teenager feel comfortable. Many competent, well-trained, and skilled psychologists, social workers, and counselors are available, but not everyone is going to be the right fit for every teenager and every family. It's worthwhile to invest some time and effort in getting a good referral and especially in interviewing a few different therapists of different types, and picking the one whose style feels most comfortable to you. When you first meet a therapist, you probably should be interviewing each other.

Once you have chosen a therapist, it's very important that you take this relationship seriously and be consistent with therapy. In all likelihood, whatever conflicts are occurring outside of the therapy session will also be played out within the therapy session with the therapist. Although it can be unpleasant at first, when this happens, it is vital that teenagers continue to go to therapy so that they can resolve these issues therapeutically. For therapy to be successful, the teenager must be willing to participate in the work of therapy and to take ownership and responsibility for how they do in therapy. If your teen really doesn't want to be in therapy, and they go in because they're being forced or cajoled into it, and they may sit there politely without being invested in the therapy work. It is true, we find, that most adolescents are not initially thrilled about therapy, and their resistance is a challenge for the therapist and the parents to overcome. A good adolescent therapist will help the parents address this issue, possibly enlisting a family therapist to support this process.

Types of Therapy

In addition to choosing a therapist, there are several different types or modalities of therapy from which to choose. The most common type is individual therapy. This is classic therapy, where the teenager sits in a therapy room one-on-one with a psychologist or social worker. They talk about their feelings and what's happened throughout the week. This is most effective for teenagers whose problems are internal, and who need help learning how to identify and express their feelings to work through some of their problems.

The next kind of therapy is family therapy. In this modality, the therapist does not work just with the teenager, but with the whole family, parents and siblings, all at once. The focus is on the structure and hierarchy of the family and the communication patterns within the family. Often, this is the most effective and efficient way of helping a teen. In fact, some Outward Bound courses are designed as family courses for just this reason. In family therapy, the therapist does not "belong" just to the teenager, but to the entire family. The therapist is neutral. Family therapy is less a place to vent your own personal feelings and frustrations as it is a place to work on and improve communication patterns between family members.

Finally, there's group therapy. In group therapy, several teenagers around the same age come into therapy together. It's less structured than family therapy, and in fact, is much closer to individual therapy. Group members talk about their own personal feelings and frustrations, and receive feedback not just from the therapist, but from the other group members as well. Discussions can range from a topic the therapist brings up to issues that individual group members bring up.

The longer we practice and the more we work with adolescents, the more we are amazed by the power and the effectiveness of group therapy.

Teenagers, by their very nature, are social creatures. It's natural, and in a lot of ways very safe, for them to be in groups. Group therapy keeps them from feeling ganged up on by adults. Rather, they feel supported by their peers in the group. They are also, often for the first time, able to feel that other people actually understand what they're going through, and may have even gone through something similar themselves. Most teenagers tell us after therapy has been completed that they found group therapy the most helpful for them. During a recent group meeting we announced that since the following week was spring break, we were assuming that the group members did not want to come to therapy, so we would cancel it for that week. After a pause, one group member raised his hand and asked since we weren't going to have group therapy, if it would be okay if the group members got together themselves anyway. The other group members nodded in agreement. That hasn't been an isolated occurrence.

Getting Your Teen Into Therapy

Teenagers may be hesitant or downright oppositional about beginning therapy. Although no strategy is perfect, here are a few ideas that might make it easier to help your teenager get involved in therapy. First, remember that once you get your teenager to the initial session and they are in the office with the therapist, you don't need to worry about this anymore. It is the therapist's responsibility to try to get the teenager hooked into therapy. Next, even if you as a parent decide that your teenager will be in therapy, it's often a good idea to suggest that the teenager interview two, three, maybe even four different therapists, and choose the one with whom they feel most comfortable. This allows them some control over the process. Of course, remember that you still have a say in the final decision, and that the final choice of a therapist must be someone with whom both they and you feel comfortable.

Secondly, you might want to try offering different options for therapy. Teens usually think of therapy as individual therapy. They often don't realize group or family therapy is available. Sometimes one of these two types of therapy will be more attractive to your teen. As we discussed earlier, group therapy feels very natural to teens. They often see it as something fun as opposed to something they *have* to do. The benefit of family therapy, on the other hand, is that the treatment is not focused solely on the teenager. Teenagers frequently feel that they're being sent into therapy because their parents view them as a problem that needs to be fixed. It's the classic, "Why should *I* have to go to therapy? I'm not the problem; you're the one with the problem" retort. Family therapy refocuses the spotlight from the teenager to the family as a whole, which makes a teenager feel that they are less to blame (or less blamed) for whatever's going on.

Finally, there's another strategy that is sometimes effective in helping to get teenagers started in therapy. Parents should invite the teenager to join them in family therapy. When the teenager says no, say, "Okay, that's your decision, but we're going anyway, and we're going to talk about you and what's been going on in the family." Without pushing, just let him know what you've been talking about in general for the first couple of weeks of therapy. After a few sessions, we often find that the teenager will ask to come into family therapy so that they can share their views with the therapist, and set everybody straight about what's *really* going on in the family. It doesn't always work, but it's worth a try.

If Your Teen Needs More Help

Medication from a psychiatrist and/or individual, group, or family therapy from a licensed therapist are all standard methods of outpatient treatment. But some teenagers require more intensive intervention than weekly or even semiweekly outpatient treatment. What options are available to these teenagers and their parents?

In an Emergency

First of all, there's your local emergency room. If you ever feel that your teenager is an immediate threat or a danger, either to himself or to others, then take him to the local emergency room. It is much better to err on the side of caution than not. As we mentioned in Chapter 10, this is a very concrete way of showing your teen that you are listening and that you care. In addition, a trip to the emergency room is not pleasant, and will show your teen that there are consequences for what he says and does. This shows that you are taking what he says seriously, and that you are going to do what is necessary to protect him.

Inpatient Treatment and Other Options

From the emergency room, teens may be admitted for an inpatient evaluation. In these days of managed health care, most inpatient stays are only about three or four days. This is long enough to help a teen get through a crisis, and to get started on a regimen of medication. After the evaluation (or in some cases, from the emergency room), they are discharged to continue their to outpatient work. In some instances, especially those in which drug or alcohol abuse plays a role, teenagers are sent to longer inpatient programs (two or four weeks), which focus specifically on the issues at hand.

As the length and frequency of inpatient treatment has decreased over the last several years, other options from the private sector have begun to emerge to meet the needs of those teenagers who need longer-term residential treatment. These options include therapeutic or emotional growth boarding schools, residential treatment centers (RTC), and therapeutic wilderness programs. Therapeutic or emotional growth boarding schools and RTCs are programs from six to nine months in length that focus on a student's social and emotional needs in addition to his or her academic progress. These schools and RTC's provide structure, support, and therapeutic interventions that are fully integrated with all other aspects of the program. The therapeutic components can include medication management; individual, group, or family therapy; and reward and reinforcement schedules. These schools provide recreation and, if necessary, academic assistance to help teenagers with academic difficulties catch up. Perhaps most importantly, these programs offer teens a change of environment, from unhealthy surroundings that led them into involvement with drugs, alcohol, or other negative influences, to an environment that is safe, nurturing, and structured, and that teaches them to make healthier decisions.

Therapeutic wilderness programs, in some ways, are very similar to Outward Bound or NOLS programs, but they integrate a formal therapeutic component into their program. These programs have Master's- and even doctoral-level therapists and psychologists out on the trail or in the woods with the teenagers, helping them gain insight into their past, take responsibility for themselves, and to learn to express their feelings, fears, and frustrations. These therapeutic wilderness programs can be an extremely powerful first step before a transition into a long-term therapeutic or emotional growth school.

Educational Consultants

Finding the right program or school can be an incredibly daunting task. As with choosing a therapist, it is less an issue of finding a good program than it is an issue of finding the program that is the right fit for your particular teenager. With both wilderness programs and emotional growth schools, there are usually several factors to consider: medication management, therapy, academic support or enrichment, structure, the actual activities that the program offers, and the general overall atmosphere. Different teenagers will need different types of interventions, and different combinations or balances, of these different factors. Thus, rather than sending away for brochures or going on the Internet to do some research on these programs yourself, we recommend that you consult a professional who has been to visit some of these schools and programs and who knows a little bit about them. It's about the same as hiring a realtor to find the best house for your needs out of what's available. But in this case, it is vitally more important to seek some professional guidance. None of us could reliably distinguish between good programs and not-so-good programs based just on a website or brochure, let alone figure out which programs would be a good fit for which particular teenagers. It is an infinitely better idea to work with a professional who has personally visited numerous programs, talked with the staff and talked with the participants in these programs privately, without the staff around. These professionals are called Educational Consultants, and their job is to interview you, your teenager, and any other individuals who might have worked with your teenager, including therapists and teachers, to clearly understand what your teenager's needs are. This person will then try to match your teenager with a school or program that will best meet his or her individual needs. They will help you with the application process, discuss financial issues, and help you transition your teenager into the program. They will also stay in contact with you while your teenager is enrolled at the program, and act as your liaison with the school or RTC. Many programs now either strongly urge or require families to work with educational consultants as a condition of acceptance.

Like the term "therapist," the term "Educational Consultant" is not a licensed term; anybody can call themselves an Educational Consultant, no matter what their credentials are. As with therapists, it's important that you find an Educational Consultant with a good background in terms of knowing the programs, but it's also vital that you choose someone you feel is going to be a good fit for your family, and someone with whom you feel you can form a good working relationship. One of the best ways to find an Educational Consultant is through an organization called Independent Educational Consultants of America (IECA, www.educationalconsulting.org). IECA will provide you with a list of certified Educational Consultants in your area.

All parents, even the best ones, need support to make sure their kids reach their potential, and even good parents sometimes need to make difficult decisions to ensure that their kids are okay. Remember that none of us can do it alone and sometimes all parents need some help and/or backup. It may not take an entire village, but at the very least, it takes a team. With the numerous different aspects and varied strengths that your teens have, it makes sense that they need numerous and varied different supports and resources.

CHAPTER 14

CHANGE IS THE ONE THING YOU CAN COUNT ON

Conclusion

If someone had asked 35 years ago what adolescent life would be like today, we doubt many people would have been able to predict the dramatic changes that have occurred in American society and how they have affected teenagers. For instance, who would have thought that the age at which most people would think that you were an adult would be 26, or that the average time it would take to graduate from college would be five to six years? Who could have foreseen Columbine? Who would have guessed that more than 50% of marriages would end in divorce, affecting millions of teenagers? Would any of us have predicted the power, prevalence, and influence of illegal drugs and early adolescent sexual activity? What about daycare nurseries in high schools and police officers and X-ray machines at school entrances? Will these trends continue, and how are we going to prepare our children and grandchildren to raise healthy, happy, productive young adults themselves?

In many cases, the bonds that began decades ago are helping families navigate these changing trends in a more complicated culture. Forty-eight percent of 18- to 29-year-olds talk or e-mail with their parents daily, and 70% of this age group reports spending time with their family in the previous week (Grossman, 2005). Clearly, parents are using their time, energy, instincts and parenting skills to help their teens step smoothly into adulthood. Parents are allowing their young adult children to return home after college when necessary and are helping them reach the next phase in their lives. Even when errors and mistakes occur, parents and their young adults are learning and growing past them.

Furthermore, just as individuals and families talk through problems in order to come to a resolution, our society is beginning to cope with many dangerous and damaging trends through dialogue and by implementing sound public policy—and it appears to be working. The divorce rate is decreasing, as is drug use in our high schools. Teenagers report that they are waiting longer before becoming sexually active, and teen pregnancy has dropped. As society recognizes and builds upon these positive changes, we hope that this progress will continue.

As we take a step back and look at the big picture for teenagers and their families, a couple of general trends come to mind:

First, communications and connections between American parents and children appear to be getting stronger, and children are remaining attached longer. The vast majority of parents love their kids deeply and are extremely committed to doing the best they can to raise healthy families. Do most parents make mistakes? Undoubtedly. (Do they make as many as we do? Hardly!) Do they learn from these mistakes and keep trying? It looks as if they do.

Second, as a rule, whether in families or societies, positive changes do not usually occur through denial and avoidance. When we become better at talking about sexuality, drug and alcohol use, the qualities and boundaries of healthy relationships, and fear of separation among other difficult topics, our youngsters become better equipped to make healthy decisions.

Finally, the only constant is change. The rate of change and the number of changes with which both teens and parents need to contend is constantly increasing. This underscores the need to proactively prepare our teens to be able to cope with the numerous and confusing changes they will encounter, and the frustration, insecurity, and anxiety that may accompany such changes. To put it another way, these changes highlight the need to focus on *process*. We must arm our teenagers with the skills they will need to negotiate, question, and adapt to these trends—and parents will need to think carefully about how to maximize their own coping, negotiation, and decisionmaking skills.

This has the potential to be an intimidating (or terrifying) thought—and it might be, if you were new at this. But you have already earned your stripes as a parent: you have gotten your child this far and you have seen a lot of this before. As you know by now, many of the issues your teen is struggling with are the same as or similar to issues you helped them with earlier in their development. The content may have changed (your 2-year-old probably didn't argue with you about dating, driving, and curfew), but the patterns and the process are the same. So these new changes can't scare you. You are a seasoned veteran. You have a teenager!

References

Alan Guttmacher Institute. (1999). *Facts in brief: Teen sex and pregnancy*. New York: Author. Retrieved 3/30/2005 from http://guttmacherinstitute.org/pubs/fb_teen_sex.html.

American Psychiatric Association. (1994). *Diagnostic and statistical manual of mental disorders* (4th ed.). Washington, DC: Author.

Grossman, Lev. (2005, January 25). Grow up? Not so fast. *Time*, 47.

Hetherington, E. M., & Kelly, J. (2003). *For better or for worse: Divorce reconsidered*. New York: W.W. Norton.

Kreider, R.M., & Fields, J.M. (2002). *Number, timing, and duration of marriages and divorces: 1996*. Washington, DC: US Census Bureau.

Natenshon, A. H. (1999). *When your child has an eating disorder*. San Francisco: Jossey-Bass.

National Women's Health Information Center. (2000). *Information sheet: Eating disorders*. Washington, DC: Author. Retrieved 3/30/2005 from http://www.4women.gov/owh/pub/factsheets/eatingdis.htm.

Schulberg, H. C., Pilkonis, P. A., & Houck, P. (1998). The severity of major depression and choice of treatment in primary care practice. *Journal of Consulting and Clinical Psychology, 66*(6).

Shisslak, C.M., Crugo, M., & Estes, L.S. (1995). The spectrum of eating disturbances. *International Journal of Eating Disorders, 18* (3), 209-219.

Siegel, M., Brisman, J., & Weinshel, M. (1997). *Surviving an eating disorder.* New York: Harper Perennial.

Sulgler, A., (1998). *Essential guide to the new adolescence.* New York: Plume Printing.

Wallerstein, J., & Kelly, J., (1979). *Surviving the breakup.* New York: Basic Books.

Wallerstein, J., Lewis, J. A., & Blakeslee, S. (2001). *The unexpected legacy of divorce: The 25-year landmark study.* New York: Hyperion.

Warshak, R. A. (2003). *Divorce poison: Protecting the parent-child bond from a vindictive ex.* New York: Regan Books.

White, K., & Speisman, J. (1977). *Adolescence.* Monterey, CA: Wadsworth Publishing.

Winnicott, D.W. (1986). The theory of the parent-infant relationship. In Peter Buckley (Ed.), *Essential papers on object relations* (pp. 233-253). New York: New York University Press.

Winnicott, D.W. (1986). Transitional objects and transitional phenomena. In Peter Buckley (Ed.), *Essential papers on object relations.* (pp. 254-271). New York: New York University Press.

For Further Reading

Barkley, Russell. (1998). *Your defiant child.* New York: Guilford Press.

Barun, K. (1989). *When saying no isn't enough.* New York: Signet Books.

Bernstein, N. (2001). *How to keep your teenager out of trouble.* New York: Workman Publishing.

Cohen, M. (1991). *Joint custody handbook.* Philadelphia: Running Press.

Conger, J. (1991). *Adolescence and youth.* Harper Collins.

Ericson, E. H. (1950). *Childhood and society.* New York: Norton.

Gurian, M. (1998). *A fine young man.* New York: Penguin Putnam.

Goleman, D. (1997). *Emotional intelligence.* New York: Bantam Books.

Hallowell, E. M., & Ratey, J. J. (1994). *Driven to distraction: Recognizing and coping with attention deficit disorder from childhood through adulthood.* New York: Simon and Schuster.

Muuss, R. (1996). *Theories of adolescence.* New York: McGraw-Hill.

Muuss, R., & Harriet, P. (1998). *Adolescent behavior and society.* New York: McGraw-Hill.

Novello, J. (1993). *Until the grownup arrives.* Hogrefe and Huber.

Rosemond, J. (1998). *Teen-proofing.* Kansas City: Andrews McMeel Publishing.

Thomas W. Stacy, PhD (left)
Dr. Stacy earned his BA and MA from Southern Methodist University and his PhD in Psychology from Texas A&M University. He has 12 years of experience as a trainer, therapist and administrator in residential treatment centers, and was both the Admissions Director and Vice President of the Discovery Land Psychiatric Hospital. For the past twenty-three years, Dr. Stacy has worked in private practice and has been the Director of Crossroads Psychological Associates in Columbia, MD. He has served on the Executive Board of the Maryland Psychological Association for the past ten years.

David A. Gold, PhD (right)
Dr. Gold earned his BA from Yale University and his PhD in Clinical Psychology from New York University. He is a former adjunct Professor of Developmental Psychology at Johns Hopkins University and was a member of the Research Psychiatry Faculty at Johns Hopkins School of Medicine. In addition to working as a School Psychologist for the Baltimore City Public School System, Dr. Gold has worked full time in private practice at Crossroads Psychological Associates in Columbia, MD for the past ten years. He is active in the Maryland Psychological Association and has served as chair of its Board of Social Responsibility. Dr. Gold has a daughter, age 6, and a son, age 2 and is awaiting payback for writing a book on teenagers.